—THE—
ENCHANTED
TAROT

THE
ENCHANTED
TAROT

CREATED BY
AMY ZERNER

WITH TEXT BY
MONTE FARBER

St Martin's Press
New York

To Ma, Jesse Spicer Zerner,
whose great love, talent, wit and wisdom
have always inspired us to be creative and helped
us to make our dreams come true.

Text copyright © Monte Farber 1990
Card illustrations copyright © Amy Zerner 1990
This edition copyright © Eddison Sadd Editions 1990

Library of Congress Cataloging-in-Publication Data
Zerner, Amy
        The enchanted tarot / Amy Zerner and Monte Farber.
        p.   cm.

"A Thomas Dunne book."
  ISBN 0-312-05079-8
  1. Tarot.   I. Farber, Monte.   II. Title
BF1879.T2Z47   1990   90-30945
133.3'2424—dc20   CIP

First US Edition

10 9 8 7 6 5 4 3

AN EDDISON·SADD EDITION
Edited and produced by
Eddison Sadd Editions Limited
St Chad's Court, 146B King's Cross Road
London WC1X 9DH

Phototypeset by Bookworm Typesetting, Manchester, England
Origination by Columbia Offset, Singapore
Printed and bound in China produced by Mandarin Offset

CONTENTS

INTRODUCTION

The "land of our dreams;" there is nothing in our lives more magical, yet more common, than this land where we all spend a third of our lives: Each night our Higher Self lovingly welcomes us home to this invisible yet omnipresent place where our waking mind's thoughts and our heart's desires are symbolically materialized along with our past, present and sometimes our future so we may be instructed, nurtured, healed and sent back to awaken, refreshed and ready to work our will in the land ruled by time and space.

Just as we know that the world does not fade away while we sleep, the land of our dreams and the incredible power of our Higher Self lives on while we are awake. This is the world contacted by people, whom we of the waking world now call "enlightened," but used to call "enchanted." The great religious mystics, prophets, seers and psychics as well as artists, inventors and all people of great creative vision seem to have been able to harmonize waking consciousness with that of the land of dreams, to produce, on a fairly regular basis, what most people sporadically experience as accurate hunches, flashes of intuition and "lucky" guesses.

Since antiquity nearly every one of these "enlightened" individuals has used a special method to contact the land of their dreams; a method that would allow them to completely occupy their mind and yet, at the same time, diffuse the focus of consciousness to the point where they are awake to both the physical world and the dream world. Religious mystics used fervent prayer, chanting, deep breathing and meditation; prophets practiced fasting and introspective isolation; seers stared into flames or danced themselves into trances; and psychics gazed into crystal balls, or employed the symbolic art appearing on beautiful tarot cards to contact the enchanted land.

The tarot is unique among these methods because each of its seventy-eight cards is designed to embody and convey a special message to both our conscious and subconscious, using only visual symbolism, the "official" language of both the land of our dreams and the visual arts.

Like our dreams, the tarot and the visual arts have the power to guide us in a way that routinely transcends differences of language and culture. Art is one of the primary methods through which it is possible to "communicate" with peoples and cultures from the near and distant past. Striking similarities of theme and myth run thread-like throughout the incredibly diverse body of the symbolic, visionary art of the people who have lived on earth. Dr Carl Jung, a psychologist (and also a student of the tarot) used this concept as the basis for his theory of the Collective Unconscious, a place where all the knowledge and emotions of everyone's past, present and future reside, eternally available to, and connecting us all, with each.other and All There Is; or if you prefer, God. Like those who have come before us, we are all citizens of the land of dreams.

This shared experience is reflected in the universality of the tarot which has relied on the artistic use of symbols since its introduction into western civilization during the time of the Renaissance, allowing not just the singularly dedicated spiritual adept, but any seeker of guidance, direct access to the wisdom and power of their Higher Self.

You can use *The Enchanted Tarot* to enter this magical realm. Rendered in the unique fabric collage style of my wife, the artist Amy Zerner, each card of *The Enchanted Tarot* is a miniature work of inspirational art worthy of meditation. The images radiate life and love and they manage to evoke the traditional meanings of the cards without the garish, violent pictures that frighten many away from the tarot. When combined with the accompanying text, the cards educate and offer guidance by uniquely and directly addressing the fundamental principle underlying the tarot: the blending of our dream-consciousness with that of our waking mind, to produce a state of enchantment.

The use of *The Enchanted Tarot* involves a novel threefold approach. Each card possesses its own special power derived from "The Dream," "The Awakening," and "The Enchantment" levels of consciousness.

THE DREAM is the gentle fable that reveals the fabric of each card's allegorical meaning by weaving a tale explaining the action and symbols portrayed. The Dream entertains as it penetrates the psyche to fulfill the card's intention. The stories are full of the innocence of youth yet they also contain the wisdom of years. Over time, repeated reading of each of The Dreams will expose deeper levels of meaning to you, as repeated viewing of the cards of *The Enchanted Tarot* will produce new insights into their purposeful design.

In each of the seventy-eight Dreams, both the twenty-two cards of the Major Arcana (traditionally numbered 0–21), as well as the fifty-six cards comprising the four suits of Minor Arcana, correspond to an archetypal dream experience. They can be seen as engaging fantasies that speak directly to our subconscious.

THE AWAKENING brings the lesson of each story into our conscious mind for evaluation and assimilation, so it may be used as a tool for guidance and personal growth. It is a straightforward explanation of what each card signifies when it appears in a specific reading.

THE ENCHANTMENT provides the link between our waking world and the land of dreams. The use of healing rituals, charms, chants and spells reinforces our awareness of the existence of the magical world and reminds us of our ability to draw on its power. These enchantments aid us in casting out fears, drawing in love and abundance, and healing emotional wounds.

The sheer beauty and unique approach of *The Enchanted Tarot* can inspire like no other. Come now as we return to the place we never leave, the place where our past is examined while our future unfolds. The land of our dreams.

THE CARDS OF
THE ENCHANTED TAROT

The Major and Minor Arcana cards of *The Enchanted Tarot* revive the ancient story-telling power of the tarot, using beautiful pictures filled with love and wisdom. This visual story-telling ability is descended from a time when only the privileged few could read. Like the cave paintings made by Neolithic tribes to teach their young the physical and spiritual attributes of local animals, *The Enchanted Tarot* has evolved from the ancient unbound, pasteboard "books" of hand-painted cards used by the wise elders to teach life lessons to the illiterate populations of India, China and, later, Europe. These lessons were also incorporated into the early religions, with various attributes and qualities deemed essential to lead a successful and harmonious life, projected onto the deities who adorned the temples. Picture cards were a convenient method of transporting and preserving the ancient traditions during pilgrimages, times of war, and of natural disasters.

The exact date of the first use of tarot cards for divination is not known. The oldest surviving deck dates from the fifteenth century, but since ancient times, it has been common to consult the oracles of various deities, whose temples and shrines are legendary for dispensing valuable advice and predictions about the conditions of life.

In this way, the wisdom of *The Enchanted Tarot* has survived because its message of a cyclical, interrelated world is strong enough to overcome both the rigors of travel through time, and the repression, persecution and ridicule the tarot has suffered at the hands of those people whose linear, mechanistic view of life has created the need for the implementation of a world-wide ecological movement.

The story of *The Enchanted Tarot* is a story of hope and faith born of the truth of the human spirit eternally seeking to know itself and its power. By meditating on the timeless truths embodied in the twenty-two cards of the Major Arcana as well as the equally important lessons applicable to everyday affairs, embodied in the fifty-six cards of the Minor Arcana, you can gain insight into the workings of the world and how to best harmonize with it your activities of both a spiritual and a physical kind.

The cards of the Major Arcana are also known as "Trump" cards, a derivative of "triumph," that refers to the fact that the cards of the Major Arcana are above those of the Minor both in order of appearance and, more importantly, spiritually. Their appearance in a reading should be regarded as important.

The cards of the Minor Arcana are divided into four suits of fourteen cards each, called Wands, Swords, Hearts and Pentacles. These suits are associated with the four elements of the ancient esoteric tradition: Fire, Air, Water and Earth respectively. There are four "Royalty" or "court" cards in each suit, a Princess, Prince, Queen and King, each symbolizing a personality type, related to the element described by each particular suit. Their appearance in a reading is an indication that the qualities of personality represented by the court card are entering your life and are to be either cultivated or avoided, according to how well the card's meaning applies to the situation and its position in the reading. Royalty cards sometimes indicate that a person of such qualities may soon appear in your life.

The suit of Wands corresponds to the element of Fire, which is associated with action, passion, creativity, enterprise, faith, the season of Spring and the direction, South.

The suit of Swords corresponds to the element of Air, which is associated with ideas, communication, truth, justice, struggles, the season of Fall and the direction, East.

The suit of Hearts corresponds to the element of Water, which is associated with emotions, moods, dreams, fantasy, romance, the season of Summer and the direction, West.

The suit of Pentacles corresponds to the element of Earth, which is associated with material possessions, labor, values, security, the season of Winter and the direction, North.

The different colors used in both the Major and Minor cards and suits of *The Enchanted Tarot* express the healing qualities relative to the respective elements and meanings assigned to all the cards.

In *The Enchanted Tarot* you have a full complement of seventy-eight oracles awaiting your sincere questions and requests. Read through each interpretation for all the cards, as you carefully study the image of each card. You will then be ready to learn the art of divination, and the cards will reveal their valuable, timeless and enchanted knowledge.

0
THE FOOL

THE DREAM

Wide-eyed and innocent as a new-born child, The Fool has descended from the celestial realms to alight on mountain tops of vibrant green and purple, ready to begin his mystical journey on the path towards enlightenment. All is new to him and he has not yet learned to fear. He lives from moment to moment, going forward without premeditated thought, unaware of the pitfalls or dangers which may lie before him. In his pouch he carries the memories, instincts and experiences of past lives, known as the "collective unconscious," waiting to be used. He carries a wand symbolizing the pure faith of his actions. It is topped with a head that looks backwards, relating The Fool's past to his present as he goes forward. The dog leaping behind him represents the animal nature of our physical bodies and is seen in playful harmony with The Fool, like a pet with a child. The dream is suffused with green, the color of growth, and the sky is filled with the clear new light of a spring season and a shining, new life. Like the court jesters who maintained his tradition, The Fool can only tell the truth for he has no malice or desire.

[handwritten note: Speak the truth & shame the Devil. —]

THE AWAKENING

Do not over-analyze things; sometimes you have to just take risks. This is not the time for sophistication or searching for hidden meanings in the words or actions of others. Be as a child or you will not see the heaven on earth. Do not look back, or attempt to anticipate actions or events. It is time for innocence and faith.

THE ENCHANTMENT

Blow soap bubbles and think of nothing. If thoughts of the world intrude, see them as soap bubbles floating by and watch them pop, one by one. Play with children and let them, not you, guide the play. Do not try to learn from these activities, just experience them. Before you take their leave, sing a round of "Ring-around-a-rosy," the ubiquitous child's game that, like the tarot itself, is a remnant of the ancient time and religions which survived persecution by hiding their wisdom in a "game."

1
THE MAGICIAN

THE DREAM

A skilled and clever magician performs an occult ritual, as energy pours from his extended right hand to erupt into a pillar of living fire. As fire can transform what is added to it, this shaman can transform one thing into another: water into steam, clay into brick, and fire into ashes. While The Fool symbolizes unconscious knowledge, The Magician is the embodiment of the conscious mind, with its ability to know and manipulate the physical world. Like The Fool, The Magician also wears a pointed hat, the apex of which alludes to the human ability to draw down cosmic forces. The Magician's hat is swathed in layers of rich fabric, just as the pure energy of a human being is wrapped in layers of flesh and blood, as well as thought and emotion. On his belt, The Magician wears a Pentacle, a Heart, a Sword and a Wand as tokens of his mastery over the four elements, Earth, Water, Air and Fire. Behind him is his heavenly city, symbol of the divine origin of desires made manifest on earth through the power of thought. The Magician is the mediator between these two worlds. With initiative and cunning, he decides which ideas will be made real.

THE AWAKENING

If your willpower is consciously and aggressively directed, you can now accomplish all that you visualize. You are challenged to go forward into the world and use your skill and intelligence, to produce change for the better. Make magic!

THE ENCHANTMENT

Prepare an altar upon a red cloth. Place a cup of water, a burning white candle, a knife, and a crystal or special rock on the cloth, to represent the four elements of the tarot. Set The Magician card among these tools. Now concentrate upon one wish that you want to manifest. Take a stick of incense in your right hand and touch it to the candle flame. Say: *"As I transform fire into ashes, so I will transform ..... into ....."* Place the incense in its holder and allow it to burn away.

2
THE HIGH PRIESTESS

THE DREAM

Under a star-spangled sky, The High Priestess of the Moon stands at the entrance of her sacred temple grotto. Passive and quiet, she represents a vessel of memory and holy female wisdom. Her powers are so great that they are almost beyond actions, and the griffon at her feet senses her desires and goes to obey her. Her timeless secrets are communicated through an inner voice, or intuition, and only those wise enough to retreat into silence will know them. Above her, perched on a crescent moon, sits an owl sacred to Athena, goddess of wisdom. The crown of The High Priestess evokes the waxing and waning moon and the natural rhythms of the female cycle. Her filmy veils and the water at her feet are symbols of the mysterious female energy that many men profess not to understand. The High Priestess effortlessly directs her psychic ability in harmony with the desires of the universe that is her child. Her hands are hidden behind the energy centers at the base of her spine and atop her head, to signify that true power comes from the use of individual spiritual energies and is available to all.

THE AWAKENING

The all-seeing spiritual sight and image of The High Priestess should be invoked and meditated upon, before the asking of any question. Her appearance is a message to go quietly within yourself, to become aware of your eternal connection to all that is, was and will be, and the strength you gain from this knowledge will bring insight.

THE ENCHANTMENT

For inner guidance and the strengthening of your psychic abilities, you must practice this enchantment on a daily basis. Close your eyes and relax. Visualize yourself in the temple grotto with The High Priestess. Know that she exists only to help you and answer your every question. While galaxies circle above you, pose your question without any attachment to the answer you will receive. In time she will take her hands from behind her back and in them will be the symbol of your answer.

3
THE EMPRESS

THE DREAM

Robed in violet, the color of the spirit, the pregnant Empress sits upon a throne of stone, rooting her to the earth. Upon her head she wears a star and halo, tying her to the heavens. In her right hand she clasps a bouquet of flowers. There are flowers all about her, for she is the fertile Earth Mother. By her unseen hand, the earth produces a cornucopia of beauty as in a well-tended garden. Her nurturing femininity helps to give birth to creative ideas. At her feet flow the waters of the "collective unconscious" uniting The Empress with her family in the most profound way. As she gazes into this misty stream, The Empress knows that its waters will give new life to the seeds that are her children. She dreams a dream that all her unconditionally loved children be fortunate and know the abundance that is their birthright. The Empress can help bring daydreams to fruition in a world where logic and intuition should dwell together as do Heaven and Earth.

THE AWAKENING

Have an open and sympathetic heart and your wishes will be provided for. Be aware of your contact; mental, emotional and physical, with the ever-new beauty, sensuality, fertility and peace of our earthly garden paradise, and you will not want for these things in your own life. Creative inspiration and productivity are available to you if you will try and bring heaven down to earth.
Exert your power with a loving hand.

THE ENCHANTMENT

To make a dream come true, take half an eggshell and balance it on a plate containing some earth. Fill the eggshell with the soil and plant a seed of your choice on the night of the new moon. As you lovingly plant the seed repeat these words: *"I will plant my dream seeds in the fertile earth of my imagination and reap a harvest of love, creativity and harmony."*

4
THE EMPEROR

THE DREAM

Beneath a tall mountain peak, The Emperor sits upon his throne. He has achieved his goals. He has climbed the mountain and even claimed it as his own but doing this has reduced the number of options available to him, thus rendering his life rather lonely. He has been a pioneer and a leader, becoming the master of all the material things he surveys. With his great reasoning abilities, he has even triumphed over passion and emotion, represented by the still water beneath him. The true patriarch, he lacks female intuition but no such "weakness" could be acknowledged by him, for fear of losing authority. Dedicated, disciplined and stable, he has no difficulty in getting others to carry out his orders. Ambitious, he will begin innovative projects that are not always as staid and conservative as he himself appears. If old patterns must be broken, he will give the matter much thought, for he wants to be perceived as benevolent and compassionate as well as infallible. Though sometimes domineering, he will always remain responsible, reliable and charismatic.

THE AWAKENING

Your attitude about acquiring and using power and authority is being tested. How do you relate to figures in authority? Act like a leader. You must take charge and use balanced, reasoned power to achieve your goal, while convincing others to help you keep your position.

THE ENCHANTMENT

On a Tuesday, pour three drops of eucalyptus oil in your right palm and anoint an unlit red candle to initiate a new project. Light it while visualizing the desired result of your ambitions. Pinch a bit of cayenne pepper onto your food for the next week. This will give you "Mars" energy and help you to assert yourself. For that week, see the whole picture clearly before you act, as if you stood atop The Emperor's mountain.

5

THE HIEROPHANT

THE DREAM

The figure of an old man, wise, placid, patient and merciful, stands on a hill offering his blessings to the union of an expensively dressed man and his equally high-born lady love. The necessary rituals of a successful family life and the society it spawns are the basis for all religions. The Hierophant, sometimes known as The Pope, represents the spiritual guidance dispensed by representatives of the traditional, organized religions. His guidance is practical and follows, without question, all dogma as taught by his predecessors. His goals are the maintaining of conventional social mores, and the assured position of his religion. The Hierophant's devotion to his position is real, as symbolized by the white heart above his head. This "father confessor" can be relied on for advice and support, within the guidelines of his training. While he faithfully lays down the codified laws and spiritual principles contained in the book he is holding in his right hand, his unremitting daily study and practice of those traditions still impart to him some of the occult knowledge upon which his religion was originally based.

THE AWAKENING

Rules and traditions are based on the sincere desire of our predecessors to preserve what was useful in their time. But your interests are not always best served by blind obedience. The repression of your right to think freely may result in conformity. Still, in many situations, religious moral values and traditions will comfort and sustain you.

THE ENCHANTMENT

Place five flat stones in a cross, one for each of the four directions: North, South, East and West, plus one in the center where you stand. Sprinkle salt water in the middle, saying: *"I consecrate this sacred place and nothing but love shall enter in. I call forth all the powers of the One Spirit to charge and attend this space."* You may now use this "church" to establish loving spiritual practices of your own design.

6
THE LOVERS

THE DREAM

In a starlit sky, Cupid hovers, telling two lovers to listen to their own hearts. There is a choice to be made, between vice and virtue. The young man puts one arm around the object of his affections but beneath them lounges a pouting, languid girl, who, driven mad by her own desires, tempts him with a more profane love, as the duality of dark and light lives within us all. Only if he is in touch with both the male and female aspects of his personality, will he make the right choice. The luminous colored rays of pure joy emanating from the energy centers along the spine of his betrothed are shining away from him, for he is blinded by his indecision. His eyes are on the other woman, almost ignoring the partner who holds him in true love's light embrace. At his foot is the same red star beneath Cupid, symbolic of the elemental lusts of the energy center at the base of the spine. He must decide to either kick it aside or trip over it. Only true love will make him whole.

THE AWAKENING

Your relationships reflect your own inner balance. Make sure that what is attracting you away from who, what and where you are now, is not a reflection of the dissatisfaction you feel with yourself. Though the card of The Lovers usually means a love affair is in progress, the choice is not always romantic or sexual but may be between any two allurements.

THE ENCHANTMENT

For resolving choices in love, take the dust of well-dried rose petals, pour it into a bag of pink silk, tie it up and hang it on a loose cord or jewelry chain around your neck. Light two pink candles and chant: *"Vice or virtue I must choose. Guide my choice so I can't lose."* Inhale the scent of the rose dust and your choice will be clear.

7
THE CHARIOT

THE DREAM

Carrying the spoils of war, a warrior maiden, Brunhilde, triumphantly wins the race. The horns of her reindeer steed and the shield behind her, symbolize the aggressive qualities that have brought her this victory. With her robust physique and stern resolve, she has harnessed not only her own considerable energies but also those of nature. Self-assurance and bravado have helped in her headlong race against formidable opposition. By suppressing all feeling and emotion, she has held onto the reins and gone forward from barren fields into green and flowering ones. The qualities that have enabled her to succeed will not always be of value in all circumstances. She must enjoy this moment of glory with the knowledge that it, like other such moments and heroines, will pass. Beneath her is a chariot symbolically rendered very small by her total conquest. Its driver also had a moment of glory, now gone forever. Only the glory of the golden unicorns on the never-reached horizon is everlasting.

THE AWAKENING

In order to triumph, you must take the reins of control and not let go. Enlist the help of the forces of nature in your quest. Right now, there is no room in your life for emotion, just single-minded concentration on your goal. But as you grow in the ability to meet life's challenges, remember to remove the defensive mask you have made for the world to see and fear.

THE ENCHANTMENT

To gain aid and protection in your race, relax, close your eyes, and see a strong, white light surrounding you, making your body appear radiant with energy and physical health. Feel yourself strengthened, both within and without. Visualize yourself accomplishing your goal and accepting the adulation of your supporters. Know that your will power and determination will lead you to victory. Use this enchantment daily, to increase your resolve.

8
STRENGTH

THE DREAM

A beautiful young princess has entered through a leafy portal into the garden in which she played as a child. Nature has held sway and now the untended garden has become overgrown. Its weeds and flowers are still beautiful, however, and she gathers both to make a harmonious bouquet. She suddenly encounters a great lioness whose paw has been caught by the tangled thorns of a rose bush that was once the pride of the garden. The fearsome animal roars loudly but the courageous young woman is not afraid. She frees the lioness and guides her with gentle control until the beast lies prostrate at her feet. The princess knows that, "the beast knows your heart's thought." She has tamed the animal's wild nature with her spiritual touch. She has no need of physical strength; by love she has conquered. The crown on the lioness signifies that she is the Queen of Beasts, and this brave, young princess is now Queen of Strength, with the sign for "infinity" crowning her highest energy center. By conquering the natural fears of her own bestial nature she has harnessed the infinite power of her spirit.

THE AWAKENING

The opposites of spirituality and carnality can be consciously brought into balance with courage and perseverance. In the face of fear, act calmly and with love and you will gain the true strength of an integrated body and spirit. At this time, force is not a match for spiritual strength. Through gentleness you will accomplish what force cannot.

THE ENCHANTMENT

Light a red candle to represent your carnal nature. Take a white candle of equal size and touch it to the burning flame. By mixing the white and red waxes together, the pink power of love will be brought into being. Let the two candles burn down together and repeat the words: *"With the loving strength of my Higher Self I will make an ally of my instinctual nature."* Keep a small piece of the pink wax with you in a sealed envelope to help you remember.

9
THE HERMIT

THE DREAM

Carrying his beautiful but strangely lit lantern, The Hermit walks the enlightened path of wisdom. He travels alone and at night, where both his robes and the dark conceal him, for his teachings are only for those who seek him out. The Hermit is a teacher who has attained profound understanding by withdrawing from the distractions of the world, in order to better contemplate the world of the mind. This kind old sage retains the wisdom of the past but is open to the new ideas of the future. All of nature takes on a special glow, revealing its secrets to the gentle curiosity of The Hermit. He is a peaceful, open-minded guide and counselor. Circumspect and introspective, he does not rush to take action or pass judgment. His advice will not be forthcoming without much consideration. A double star shines upon his path, providing the light of conscious and unconscious minds; the source of all knowledge. If this solitary provider of wisdom is followed with reverence, and without the desire for materialistic goals, he will shed much light on any problem.

THE AWAKENING

Do not look outside yourself for the answer. It is time to withdraw and follow your inner light. Some introspection may lead to self-improvement. With mature deliberation, things will be resolved. A person may appear, drawing upon their life experience, in order to help you. Prudence may dictate that all answers are not revealed immediately.

THE ENCHANTMENT

Choose a book that you feel has guided you with wisdom and insight in the past. Hold it in your lap. Place in a bowl earth or stones from a nearby path or road. Upon its surface sprinkle a pinch of golden glitter dust. Light a blue candle. Now quietly open the book to any page. Read it where your eyes fall first. You will find the guidance you have requested.

10
WHEEL OF FORTUNE

THE DREAM
The "wheels within wheels" that make up the Wheel of Fortune, spin and turn like the never-ending rhythms and cycles of life. A spin of the wheel may bring unexpected luck, opportunity and good fortune or it may cause the reverse, and present obstacles to our desires. A confrontation with some action from the past may occur with a turn of the wheel. Is this "Fate," "God's Plan," or "Karma?" What seem to be beginnings and endings are in fact merely part of the seamless circle of life. Rising up from the horizon are two puffs of smoke that symbolize the form of spirit. In spite of all the changes, nothing remains but the elusive spirit. The graceful peacocks spreading their tails represent expansion and wealth. The lively golden horse raises its hoof with the excitement of taking a risk, of betting and winning. An eagle soars high above, symbolizing the feeling of supremacy gained by reaching the top of the wheel. Up above reigns a Sphinx, with glowing eyes that see all the cycles, recurring patterns and evolutions. She knows that no one stays on top forever.

THE AWAKENING
The turning Wheel of Fortune is a message that what goes around, comes around, or, what goes up, must come down. You will reap what you have sown, thus you must think ahead and consider your actions, whether you find yourself on top or at the bottom of the wheel. To avoid being ruled by Fate, take responsibility for your life and what happens to you. Take risks. Be open to any new or unexpected opportunity.

THE ENCHANTMENT
Perform this enchantment during a new moon. Light three orange altar candles and some incense, to fill the air with a sweet scent. Meditate on the Wheel of Fortune card, with its wheels spinning round and round. Chant: *"Goddess of Fortune, please hear my plea, Goddess of Fortune, please come to me."* Know that by the full moon you will experience good luck.

11
JUSTICE

THE DREAM

With a face possessing the innocence of youth, and the wisdom of years, a winged messenger bears the ultimate truth. Her heart-tipped, star-encrusted spear – a mixture of the Heart, Pentacle, Wand and Sword of the Minor Arcana – will cut through the outer layer of obscuring veils to reveal the simple truth, hidden at the core. This bright blade will mete out a deserved punishment, or protect and defend valid beliefs. The scales held in the angel's right hand are used to weigh all factors to find the balance between truth and justice. The angel of Justice is *not* blind but does see all the sides of any given question. Beyond this impartial angel, a pink sky indicates the dawn of a new day which will reveal even higher moral values. Justice is implacable; in the search for truth, Justice will always prevail. The angel stands on a huge leaf, symbolizing the natural, ordered calm that Justice brings to a world of apparent chaos. Without her, no kingdom can endure for long.

THE AWAKENING

Now is the time for reason and for being able to see another's viewpoint. It is time for balancing accounts, on a physical, mental and emotional level; and in financial and legal matters. Make preparations to reap what you have sown. Have faith that Justice will triumph, and leave the punishment of those you think have wronged you in her wise and fair hands.

THE ENCHANTMENT

Burn some dried sage leaves in a metal dish to clear the air of negativity. Write down on a square of white paper, the truth of the balanced outcome you desire. Close your eyes and pray to the angel of Justice to decide the best outcome for all parties, saying: *"Open our eyes and the truth shall rise."* Open your eyes and burn the paper with some more dried sage. Know that in the end Justice always triumphs.

12
THE HANGED MAN

THE DREAM

Under a calm, blue sky and above the radiant, flowering earth, a man hangs upside down, suspended by one foot from the tail of a dragonfly. The dragonfly emphasizes that this scene is not one of torture, but part of a natural process. The young man's life is in limbo but his face shows only acceptance and absolute faith at this moment of total surrender to a higher force. He seems to be listening to an inner voice. He may be looking for an answer that is completely opposite to all he has previously believed. Perhaps he has deliberately sacrificed himself to attain some desired goal. He could be in a trance, or in a state of illumination as a result of the increase in blood flowing to his head. It does appear, however, that the pattern of his everyday life has been reversed to provide a new outlook. The water flowing beneath symbolizes that the young man has risen above emotional turmoil to accept this suspension of his usual way of life. The enforced period of waiting may be viewed as a way of gaining new perspective.

THE AWAKENING

New perspectives are required. This period in your life may seem restrictive but you are being forced to become more introspective, to listen to your higher mind. Waiting has its place in any plan. Try not to become a martyr but do not be afraid to make sacrifices or be unwilling to adapt to changing circumstances. If you feel powerless, blocked or stuck in a rut you must "lift yourself up by your own bootstraps."

THE ENCHANTMENT

The word "yoga" means "union." Try the following yoga posture, called The Bow. Lie face down on a mat or a rug. Reach behind you with both hands and grasp your ankles. Slowly raise your trunk and legs at the same time, as high as you comfortably can. Hold this position for fifteen seconds. The flow of energy circulating through your body will direct and focus your mind.

13
DEATH

THE DREAM

The King of Death is smiling. His stance is somewhat tentative, as if he might begin to dance at any moment. His skeletal form is a reminder that death exists within life. His posture and smiling face reveal that new life will come from death. Death does not want to be feared, for he stands for transformation, re-birth and renewal and for the end that comes to all things. The superficial has been pared away; all the desires of the flesh have been banished. Death walks in a universal garden of vibrant, fiery flowers, next to a life-giving stream under a sky whose stars are linked together, by their common fate. With the cutting away of old growth, new growth arises. When transition occurs, there is a new beginning. An act of release can make it possible to move forward once again. Though there is profound change, it is part of the cycle of renewal and re-birth, and can be seen as a form of liberation. To fear Death is to fear life. We truly live by living in harmony with Nature's laws.

THE AWAKENING

There is going to be profound change which, if resisted, may be painful. If the ending is unhappy, let it go and move forward. Seek the essentials of the matter, ignoring all superfluous detail. Destroy old patterns to reveal a new, rewarding path. Do not fear change or passing away. Your fear of Death must be recognized and confronted before it is allowed to interfere further with your enjoyment of life.

THE ENCHANTMENT

If you are having trouble dealing with change, place a bunch of newly-cut flowers in a vase. Over the next thirteen days, observe them as they wither and die. Take them to a burial site and whisper these words as you cover them with earth: *"Old flowers, new flowers, release my soul, renew my powers."* Let go of your pain and walk away.

14
TEMPERANCE

THE DREAM

An angel is teaching a woman the patience and discipline necessary to hold up the jar and pour life-giving water into the bowl containing the four elements, without spilling a drop. Above them, the celestial clock marks the perpetual, regular movement of life and seasons. Time is the essential, yet invisible ingredient in the "alchemy" required to change the "lead" of present circumstance into a "golden" future. The success of the experiment will depend not only upon how well the various ingredients of circumstance are blended but on the attention and patience shown to ensure that everything is mixed at the right time. At the angel's feet is a full-grown bonsai tree whose perfect beauty is the result of time and the cooperation between human and natural intelligence. The woman must learn to successfully blend the opposing factors and polarities in her life. The angel appears as an example of the beneficial synthesis of the spiritual and material world.

THE AWAKENING

The size or quality of your plans is not the issue; patience and timing are the keys necessary to unlock the treasures of the future. Now is the time for moderation. You can experiment, as long as you are in harmony with practical considerations and natural laws. You should always temper justice with mercy. Like tempered steel, your decision will be much stronger and more permanent.

THE ENCHANTMENT

To help you to endure the inevitable delay attached to anything that is worth waiting for, combine the following essences to keep your energies in harmonious balance. To a cup of warm, spring water, add two teaspoons of apple cider and one teaspoon of honey. As you sip it think: *"I am patiently healing myself in preparation for the time that will soon be here."*

15
THE DEVIL

THE DREAM

This is the face of evil. Blinded to his spiritual nature The Devil looks down on his treasures, his slitted eyes in complete obsession with and surrender to the material world. His ill-gotten gains are of no real use to him though, because his fraud and trickery have driven all companionship away. The Devil expresses the worst side of human nature; following decadent impulses blindly and judging things only for their surface value. This is the dark side of the soul, ignorant of what is real and valuable. The Devil, with his scarlet lips and black horns, is the creature of nightmares and paranoia. Under his influence, fear of the unknown becomes haunting. Restless undercurrents flow, irritating the appetites and demanding instant gratification. All love is lacking in The Devil for he views it as a sign of weakness. Though he may simply be mischievous at times, he will try to take advantage of any situation and cannot be trusted. He sets free only those who choose to see beyond their own material desires.

THE AWAKENING

If you need material objects to make you feel good about yourself, then you must feel empty and afraid that you will be recognized as such. You need to change the emphasis from physical concerns, to those of the spirit. Your bondage is the result of your limited beliefs about the world. You have within you the power to change your beliefs, using visualization, affirmations and actions in harmony with the natural law. You don't have to resort to deceit.

THE ENCHANTMENT

You may need some spiritual cleansing now. Crystals have power to help heal and balance us. Choose either clear quartz or amethyst. Purify the crystal by washing it with salt water. Wipe it dry with a silk cloth. Hold it to your lips and chant: *"I wish to transcend my obsession. Help me to see love where I see temptation."* Place the crystal on The Devil card.

16
THE TOWER

THE DREAM

Lightning has struck and is still crackling in the midnight sky. A strong, old structure has been explosively blown apart. The security afforded by this splendid monument to human endeavour has been reduced to ruin by the forces of natural law. Flames erupt and smoke fills the air; there has been a dramatic reversal of fortune. Plans for the future have been aborted. In the village below The Tower's mountain base, the people question whether the old order can survive. The explosion has a liberating potential; it has cleared a site for new growth. This may appear as a "bolt from the blue," like sudden insight that can produce immediate change. But there can be an almost inevitable and even unpleasant period of transition when there is a cataclysmic change. Emotions may erupt in anger and shock. Both physical and mental therapy may be necessary, in order to achieve freedom. Lightning has struck, but enlightenment may follow.

THE AWAKENING

Mounting pressures must be released or there will be a sudden reversal of all the work carried out so far. There has been a dramatic turn of events and established patterns of thought will be changed. It may or may not have been inevitable, but this explosion of old, perhaps false values, can be beneficial. Placing exclusive faith in material objects can lead to disaster, because only the spirit is eternal.

THE ENCHANTMENT

Use this enchantment to lessen the destructive nature of necessary changes. Take an egg. Carefully write the story of your situation around the egg from its top to its bottom. As you cup the egg in both hands, chant three times: *"Change my life but keep me calm, change will come but I'll go on."* Smash the egg and then clap your hands.

17
THE STAR

THE DREAM

There is peace after a storm. A star of hope and wonder shines in the heavens, promising spiritual illumination and inspiration. Below, with one foot on the land and the other poised magically on the surface of the stream of the unconscious, a nearly-naked maiden stands entranced. She is joyously receiving the waters of the pond, which rise up to her from an enchanted water lily while she pours an endless shower of stars from her two cupped hands, back into the flower. She shows that as heaven nourishes the earthly universe, the beauty of the physical world nourishes heaven. The star in her hair is truly a star upon which to wish for little miracles, with the guilelessness of a child. The response will be love, beauty, peace and help of all kinds. In the realm of The Star all is fresh and new, all is innocence. The maiden's language is poetry and art as she is in perfect accord with her spiritual gift. The Star is a reminder that after the storm of life's upheavals, there is a cleansing and purifying time when a sense of wonder heralds new belief that dreams can come true.

THE AWAKENING

Take time to recharge yourself with a period of relaxation. Enjoy being "the star" of your own life story. This is a time for the quiet excitement and pure enjoyment of spiritual ideas and concepts. Let your ideas pour out to nourish those you love. Let your mind dwell on what is good and pleasant in your life and avoid negativity for a while. It is important that you express your creative urge by either making or enjoying art.

THE ENCHANTMENT

Cut out a star the size of your hand, from a sheet of pale blue paper, on the night before a full moon. Place it under a glass of water and leave it there until the night following the full moon. Drink the water and think: *"As I drink this water, I am inspired by the moon and stars."* Close your eyes and receive a message. Write it down on the star and keep it safe.

The Goddess who cares for all

18
THE MOON

THE DREAM

Under a waning moon, in a dark and eerie landscape, a lost child stands with her faithful dog. She gazes up fearfully at the moon, remembering terrifying stories of a Moon Witch who plays cruel tricks on those lost in the night. She raises her hands, as if in prayer, and hopes that she will be saved and guided through this nightmare. Across a moat of turgid water, inhabited perhaps by fearsome things, she suddenly sees the turrets of her castle home. But the drawbridge is up, the gates are locked and no one seems to hear her cries. Has the Moon Witch's magic barred her way home? Just as the child is about to succumb to overwhelming feelings of despair, danger and the sadness born of longing for home and family, The Moon beams out more strongly from behind the clouds and suddenly appears warm yet pensive. The Moon is crying because she has so wrongly been thought to be a malicious Moon Witch. Tears from this pale-faced goddess fall into the water and suddenly the land swells up higher than the moat and the gate surrounding the castle. The child clearly sees the way home as she gives thanks to The Moon.

THE AWAKENING

This is the darkness before the dawn. You must separate illusion from reality. Even though the path may seem frightening and treacherous, you need not fear the mysterious unknown. Your intuition can guide you to hidden opportunities. Remember to save your energies for the challenges ahead and not squander them with anxious worrying.

THE ENCHANTMENT

Outside, under a waning moon, visualize a circle of protective light around yourself as you stand by a body of water. Hold a black stone in your hands. Concentrate and project a specific, personal fear into the stone. Then strongly hurl it out of your circle of light into the pond, lake, stream or ocean as you chant:
"With this stone, fear be banished, into water it has vanished."

19
THE SUN

THE DREAM

A pair of birds ask for and receive a life-giving blessing from The Sun before they begin to build their love nest. In appreciation, the birds promise to sing The Sun's praises every morning, when he returns from his journey below the Earth. The radiant Sun, like that drawn in corners of pictures by children all over the world, symbolizes the divine child within every individual. In the idyllic scenes from childhood, everything is open and always flooded with The Sun's rays. There are no boundaries and no secrets. Earthly pleasures, good cheer and success all seem to beam down, as paternal energy radiates from The Sun's smiling face. The seven rays emanating from the all-seeing Sun represent the seven basic colors of the color spectrum. Seven is also the traditional number of good fortune. The supremely generous Sun gives us the gift of the four seasons and, most of all, springtime with a freshly colored, re-born Earth. Each morning he brings new light to banish the haunting, formless shapes of the night.

THE AWAKENING

Everything will be sunny and bright. Love, friendships and relationships of all kinds are highlighted. It is a time to emulate The Sun's active, creative ability to realize new works of art and love. Be a dynamic, inspiring and influential leader whose light shines for all to see. Show the world who you are and what you have done. Express yourself so that everyone you encounter can feel your warmth.

THE ENCHANTMENT

At either sunrise or mid-day on a Sunday, arrange a bunch of brightly colored flowers and prepare a goblet of sparkling mineral water mixed with orange juice. Adorn yourself with jewelry and a golden garment. On a yellow ribbon write these words: *"Golden light, we are one, shine on me, gift of The Sun."* Tie it around your wrist and drink the "sun-water." Enjoy the day.

20
JUDGMENT

THE DREAM

High in a dawn sky filled with violet light, a heavenly herald is blowing his trumpet to announce the coming of the highest level of Judgment. This is not a time for punishment and retribution but a time of being called to account for past actions and experiences. The angelic herald is calling upon us to remember the life of the spirit, where the lives of all who live beneath the Moon and Sun are important. From the dark, clouded waters of emotion, a hand, wearing the ring and cuffs that show attachment to the material world, reaches upwards into the rarefied air of the higher plane. With deliberate effort, a positive move is being made. The past has been reflected upon; positive resolution will be reinforced. With atonement and repentance, real advancement occurs with the attainment of the spiritual goals. The distant green hills hint at the possibility of a new life of vitality and achievement.

THE AWAKENING

From deep within the core of your being comes a call announcing that it is time to make an important change. No matter how you have been caught up in the affairs of the world, you must evaluate past actions, become more aware of who you are and what your ultimate goals should be. You may be reluctant to admit the necessity for change but you should listen to the call of the spirit. You are *who* you are and not what you do for a living.

THE ENCHANTMENT

Have a bell or horn of some kind at hand. Imagine that it could wake up what has been dormant inside you and chant: *"The tide has turned, the light has come, on this new day we are reborn. A time for change, a whole new plan, I have no fear of Judgment's hand."* Sound the bell or horn to signal the coming of guidance from your higher self.

21
THE WORLD

THE DREAM

A copper statue of a woman has come to life and is dancing, looking back at a leaf she holds in her outstretched hand. Just as the earth, divine Mother of us all, evolved from the stars and materialized into reality, so have our bodies been created out of Her naked body, so we may dance the dance of life just as She dances through the cosmos. The statue's copper body has been dug from the earth as raw ore, refined by processes discovered by human intelligence and animated by the electrical spark that animates all life. She looks back at the leaf – a smaller version of the large leaf at her feet from which she has just emerged – to remind herself that she, like all of us, is a product and a process of the natural world. She dances before a huge image of the Earth suspended by flower petals over a columned temple, just as we all must assume our place in relationship to the Sacred Temple that is the Earth before our bodies return to Her in an ever-turning cycle. This dream-like journey is one of going within and finding our essential harmony with All There Is. When we attain the knowledge of who we really are we gain The World.

THE AWAKENING

By uniting and balancing your long-sought inner harmony with the skills you have learned in life you have achieved real success. The World can be yours in this situation. Hard work is demanded to attain this but material rewards and inner peace are promised. You must view your life in the context of the whole of life itself, before you will have the knowledge you seek.

THE ENCHANTMENT

Form a circle with a group of friends. Hold hands. Slowly move in a clock-wise direction, dancing and swaying to this chant: *"Winter, Spring, Summer, Fall. The World is dancing, dance for all."* Complete the circle twenty-two times. Close your eyes. Visualize the Earth in the center of your circle, bathed in white light, receiving the love and the healing energy from your group. Know that we all are blessed with the sacred duty of being caretakers of our Mother Earth.

ACE OF WANDS
INITIATION

THE DREAM
The power of pure energy streaks in vivid colors behind a burning torch. Blue lightning bolts erupt to awaken one to the self's own reality and vitality. The blue spring flower at the base of the card tells us that in this dream everything is as spontaneous as a spark igniting a blazing fire. Anything negative, anything that holds us back, can be burned away leaving a new beginning – our personal springtime. The phoenix arises from the ashes. The flowers above the stars at the base of the card, with their plumes of smoke, show this new growth. The stars add the inspiration of the universe, where new worlds burst into being, and comets race in blazing glory. The woman's hand has been tattooed with images of the first growth of leaves from newly sprouted seeds; between the knuckles of her index and middle fingers is the image of a winged heart. This is the pure love that is at the heart of all life. This basic, unfettered impulse of life – the desire to experience the warmth of creativity, consciousness, sexuality, enlightenment and bliss – is like a club to break down the cold wall of darkness and non-being. The club is the unifying background shape on all the cards of the Wands suit.

THE AWAKENING
At this moment, you feel alive, creative and passionate. If you don't accept this instant when it arrives, it may be lost. Use your instincts during this time of impulse and enthusiasm. It is time to initiate new projects. Do not question your power to do so. Go by your first impression and do not second-guess yourself.

THE ENCHANTMENT
Gather flowers of yellow and orange. Place them in a shallow, clay bowl and set it in a sunny location. When the flowers have dried, powder them with a pestle. Add a few drops of scented oil and burn them as an offering before one yellow candle. As you light the candle repeat: *"Power and passion are inspired. Fear and darkness are retired."*

TWO OF WANDS
PLANNING

THE DREAM

After a long climb, a man stands alone on a mountain top leaning on his staff. There are no signs of fatigue; he has simply paused, strong and upright, for a moment of contemplation. He calmly deliberates the balanced choice of the four directions, shown by the two crossed wands above him. In this peaceful moment of rest, he is aware of his own power and abilities as the land below is his dominion. He alone has inherited this place and is now ready to assert himself. There are no doubts to plague him because he has balanced both the masculine and feminine sides of his self, thus obtaining true power. The future appears as a time of growth and renewal. He carries the tools, and the knowledge of how to use them, to ensure his future is a bright one. The butterfly symbolizes his thoughts for new directions and explorations. He is strong and confident in his expectations. Free, for a time, of the distractions in the valley below, he can now decide his course of action.

THE AWAKENING

You have become established and independent. Because you are now in a position of decision-making power, the fears that you have experienced in the past no longer hold sway. This is a time to map out your plan before you are forced to return to the day-to-day reality of working out the details. You can be master of all you survey.

THE ENCHANTMENT

Lie face-down on the ground, placing your palms flat upon the earth, and resting your face on your hands. Be aware of the look, texture and smell of the soil. Relax and let the earth's powerful strength flow up through you, literally "grounding" you. Repeat: *"Let the strength of the earth fill me, let it renew me, and help me grow in full abundance."*

THREE OF WANDS
OPPORTUNITY

THE DREAM

Three cupids, representing heart, mind, and action, have spontaneously joined together. These "bearers of opportunity" sense the dynamic energy of the imminent realization and manifestation of a wish. Red flowers and flames symbolize the energy and light available at this time of creative invention. The special joy that comes with the fearless self-expression of life retains the purity and innocence of childhood, where all things are new. Two of the cupids – one with his eyes closed – hold the three wands aloft, while the third, in his excitement, has almost let go of his share of responsibility. They are playfully acting out the message that without clarity of vision, cooperation and concentration, this opportunity might come to naught. Their attitude is one of caution; to use this fateful moment of joyful awareness and creativity wisely.

THE AWAKENING

Adopt an attitude that allows you to see directly as a child, and look for "playmates" or soulmates, for collaboration in a happy enterprise. Let this moment of openness be joined with practicality and find others who, in union, will each add specific skills for a successful conclusion to a shared venture. Now is the time to sow the seeds of future harvests.

THE ENCHANTMENT

Using brightly colored crayons, draw a picture of what you need or wish to manifest. Place the drawing under three orange candles on a new moon. Light the candles. When the candles have burned out, an opportunity should present itself. Remember to look with the eyes of a child, because if you look only for the shape you expect your opportunity to take, you might not see it.

FOUR OF WANDS
COMPLETION

THE DREAM

This is a time of ceremony and celebration. The wands support a fruitful tree, heavy with the results of perfected skills and work well done. Beneath the tree are joined a husband and wife. They are richly dressed and there is a suggestion of domestic tranquillity, security and mutual support as they stand back-to-back, and shoulder-to-shoulder, with their feet firmly planted. Together they have achieved much and their harmonious relationship has helped to bring forth this harvest. Calm lines of structured energy traverse the sky. The tree itself is topped with a golden <u>finial</u> to cap the success of their aspirations and the happiness of their relationship. Two birds perch above the pair, singing a song of thankfulness to the world and carrying the message that all is well. The wands are rainbow colored, symbolizing that this good fortune will not be destroyed.

ornament

THE AWAKENING

Enjoy the satisfaction of a job well done. Your labors have not only created a strong foundation, but the hard work done to meet your obligations and the effort required to produce your best have resulted in an optimistic, proud and thankful celebration.

THE ENCHANTMENT

Create a special feast to honor the completion of a project. Decorate the table with a bowl of apples, flowers and grains of the season. Attach a special message of gratitude to each guest on each apple. As you finish your meal, have each guest give thanks for their own personal "harvest." Then pass your surprise around and let your guests eat their special apple and know how much you appreciate their association with you.

FIVE OF WANDS
COMPETITION

THE DREAM

Under five crossed and opposing wands, two leaders of compet-
ing forces face each other. They have reached an impasse. There
has been much quarreling, and finally armed combat, but these
warriors still respect each other as all men of war honor a worthy
opponent. They are equally paired and neither one is willing to
concede defeat as each holds his point of view to be correct. In
their confrontation, there is much energy that is held back.
Although angry and frustrated, they are restrained in their
dealings with one another, hoping that they still may win by
making the other admit his errors of judgment. If wisdom
prevails, this struggle can remain balanced and perhaps, even-
tually, these stubborn soldiers will be able to compromise and
accommodate each other's point of view. The circle above them
represents a higher plan which has not yet been revealed.

THE AWAKENING

In this world of competition and conflicting views, stand up for
yourself and your ideas. Refuse to be a victim. But in a frustrating
situation, try to be creative instead of restrictive. The struggle
should be fair and representative of all points of view. If your
sense of self is strongly defined and manifested, do not let this
deny others a forum for their own ideas. Do not fail to express
your own ideas with clarity and logic.

THE ENCHANTMENT

Under a new moon, cut out a circle of paper the size of your fist.
Cut it in half. On one half, write a list of your points of view in red.
On the other half write down your opponents' points in blue. Now
tape the circle back together and hold it up to the sky saying: *"I
don't see the moon, though I know it is there. I don't see the
end of this strife, though I know it is there. Two parts of a
whole are equal."* Burn it.

SIX OF WANDS
VICTORY

THE DREAM

Against a splendid fiery sunset, a triumphant young man on horseback appears. His great horse leaps forward on a tide of energy represented by the sacred flames below. On his head he wears a ceremonial headdress of victory. For a supreme instant, this rider is a victor, experiencing his exaltation on all four levels; mental, physical, emotional and spiritual. He is filled with honor and pride, a confident conqueror who knows that through his leadership, and in rising completely and instinctively to the occasion, he has won the day. This victory is represented by a blazing, shooting star lighting up the sky in a moment of intense, if brief, glory. The silver wands gleam in its reflected fire which, even if quickly extinguished, will always be remembered.

THE AWAKENING

Victory is approaching. Have faith that you will win. The spotlight is upon you. Accept this time of recognition and growth, as you have triumphed in a difficult situation. Things will work out favorably if you persevere in a time of crisis. Remember to use this victory to make a firm foundation on which to build future successes. Include those who have been of help to you in your celebration.

THE ENCHANTMENT

Make a wreath of laurel or ivy and hang it above your bed along with a piece of paper upon which these words are written: *"North, East, South, West, I am victorious, I am the best."* Keep these symbolic tokens from one full moon to the next, reciting the words on the paper each morning and night. Then burn them and strew the ashes along the four corners of your residence.

SEVEN OF WANDS
COURAGE

THE DREAM

A lone, but stalwart figure stands defiantly in front of the battlements. He could retreat behind the stone walls to protect himself but courageously he has taken this challenge. His face is determined, his shield held high, and his magical staff is more than equal to the seven flaming wands arrayed against him. At his feet, a great red blossom flowers, embodying all the things he has nurtured and cared for – loved ones, the land and all living things upon it. He firmly believes that values and ideas long established, tested and supported, must be defended. If justice is not forthcoming, he alone will resolve all difficulties. He knows that he can hold his own by confronting his problems directly. When challenged in the extreme, he cannot compromise.

THE AWAKENING

You are challenged to stand by your beliefs and values. Do not be afraid to personally defend what must be defended. Only by being assertive will you win the day. Trust your judgment and intuition and believe that, even if the situation looks forbidding and difficult, you will know how to handle it. Remember that the difference between heroic and cowardly behavior is that a hero or heroine goes forward in spite of fear.

THE ENCHANTMENT

Tuesday is ruled by Mars who gives us courage and determination. On a Tuesday, write this inscription upon a smooth stone with a permanent marker to create a talisman: *"Courage of Land, courage of Sea, strengthen, fill and favor me."* Keep your talisman a secret and carry it with you, touching it to empower you in times of need.

EIGHT OF WANDS
SIGNALS

THE DREAM

A young woman stands before a fiery rose. Eight other flowers rise heavenward, like the puffs of smoke used as smoke signals. The woman has conjured up this beautiful fire by quickly rubbing her hands together until a spark sprang to ignite the rose. This spark symbolizes action and information passing from one place to another, generating light and heat in the process. The fast-moving wands emanating from the smoke signal flowers, are traveling both towards the woman and towards her objective. Everything is very direct and in motion, suggesting fast progress. Now is the time for the woman to initiate swift action; to send and receive messages and signals, whether of love or new ideas. She knows that time is of the essence, because the flames of romance will not burn forever unless they are fed by mutual declarations of love.

THE AWAKENING

Do it and do it now. Action is demanded if the things you wish for are to be attained. Initiate communication first and the answering messages will come back to you. Make that call. Act on that new idea. The time is right to respond to the needs of the moment in the most direct way possible. Messages of love and romance are highlighted. Perhaps it is time to tell someone you love them.

THE ENCHANTMENT

Stand in an open place and light a stick of sandalwood incense. Face north and blow a little smoke in that direction. Turn east, south and west and do the same in each direction. Visualize the signals you want to send or receive all the while you chant: *"Wish to heaven now ascend. Time of waiting at an end."*

NINE OF WANDS
DISCIPLINE

THE DREAM

A confident goddess-like woman stands on a stone pedestal holding aloft two chevron-tipped wands, through the sheer strength of her will. She is preparing to send them flying, tip-first, into the ground, as she has already done with the other seven wands, to complete a barrier of protection at the mouth of her cave. She hesitates to complete the job, realizing that she may be as much a prisoner of her efforts as she will be secure. This is the dual nature of discipline. The flower above her, however, radiates sun-energy and health of mind and body, so she will make the choice most appropriate to the situation. Her decision may be at variance with commonplace judgments and moralities, but she is not swayed by the opinions of the multitudes. She is always ready to face opposition strengthened by the courage of her convictions. Her base is secure.

THE AWAKENING

You must gather and maintain great strength in reserve. Prepare to defend your position, even if it is unpopular with those you respect. You may have to bide your time but you must stay faithful to your purpose. Apply techniques of strict military-like discipline to the development of your strength of will, character and body because the time of challenge approaches. Just remember to temper your strength with the knowledge that it is to be used to meet a challenge.

THE ENCHANTMENT

To ensure a successful outcome, sit perfectly still in a spot you consider to be one of your places of power, and say this prayer: *"Lord of Light and Life, I call upon you in my hour of need. I have chosen a course of action. Grant me the strength to prepare and endure."*

TEN OF WANDS
OPPRESSION

THE DREAM

A lone workman in a dark, enclosed space carries a heavy, smoldering burden. Overwhelming everyday responsibilities have almost become unbearable. Although a physically strong man, he appears ready to collapse. A cloud of smoke hangs over him, affecting his concentration and obscuring his field of vision. There is a feeling of complete exhaustion erasing all emotion, making it impossible to exert any power or to express himself. He should be able to rest or reconsider his problems but he may feel that he is under someone else's control and cannot do anything. Could these responsibilities and this suffering be a Karmic debt? At any rate, he appears to have taken on too much and will be forced finally to concentrate on the things that he barely has the strength to pursue.

THE AWAKENING

When you have over-committed yourself, everything becomes a strain. The resulting fatigue leaves you unable to express your thoughts and drained of power. Take the time to think through your predicament, if you are lucky enough to be able to do so. Define your real goals stripped of all extraneous distractions. In this way, tensions will be released and your limited energies put to their best use.

THE ENCHANTMENT

Prepare a bath of steaming water and add a few drops of pine oil. Light a green candle, consecrated for healing, and, after the water cools sufficiently, bathe in the candlelight. Massage your temples and breathe in the vapors. Imagine your tensions being cleansed away. For the time being, think only of the water, the pine-scented air and the gently flickering flame. This brief, but potent respite will enable you to once again take up your burden with renewed hope for the future. Remember: *"This too shall pass,"* the only sentence that is always true.

PRINCESS OF WANDS

THE DREAM

This Princess of the Palace of Fire is enthusiastic and courageous. A charming and boyish type of lass with auburn hair, she
is impulsive in either love or anger. She can be blunt to the point
of being tactless, for she lacks the wisdom born of the maturity of
years. The brilliance and energy she brings to ventures will carry
others along with her but sometimes her enthusiasm can be
short-lived and burnt up quickly. This makes for a certain amount
of instability as the energetic speed of the moment may dissipate
and seem to suddenly reverse into anger or theatrics. Fire-red
butterflies whirling about represent her ever-present thoughts
and ideas. The jaunty feather-flame in her hat can be used as a
pen to write down spontaneous flashes of inspiration. Her free,
liberated spirit moves in new directions without fear and masters
all internal blocks. This winning adventuress is associated with
news and inspiring information, usually from relatives or friends.

THE AWAKENING

An opportunity may be coming your way. You must balance your
need to be rash and impetuous with the necessity of acting in a
mature, steady manner. Wild at times and easily fired up, the
Princess of Wands awakens us to the enthusiastic and spontaneous side of life. Be aware that the appearance of the Princess
of Wands in a reading may mean that a person with her qualities
will soon be appearing in your life.

THE ENCHANTMENT

Write in red ink on yellow paper the first wish that comes into
your head, no matter how childish it may seem. Burn it in a
cauldron with a sprinkle of sesame seeds. As it burns, quickly say:
*"Princess of Wands, your friend I be, join me in saying, Open
Sesame!"* Know that she will communicate with the Fates about
granting your wish and bring a new burst of growth and activity
to your day.

PRINCE OF WANDS

THE DREAM

The dark Prince of Wands rides into view upon his great, plumed charger, carrying a fire-tipped wand. Behind him the gray, dusky clouds swirl like smoke, against which his figure glows like red embers. His journey is carrying him into the unknown but he is a pioneer and filled with energy and excitement. He likes to take risks. An active, unpredictable and competitive disposition drives him forward. He radiates a very masculine energy, full of creativity and passion. His youth, however, sometimes impels him to be quarrelsome or overbearing if he feels his authority and leadership are in question. Somewhat self-centered, he is likely to think he knows a good deal more than he does. Ever restless and ambitious, he looks for a change of residence or to move up in the world. Wishing to climb higher, he hopes to meet people in his travels who will further his ambitions.

THE AWAKENING

There is a message here about a change of residence or a change of job. In making this move you will meet someone who sparks a creative urge. This will be an opportunity to expand your effectiveness in the world through courage and endurance. Original thinking will be a strong asset. Be careful not to boast too much about your successes. Be aware that the appearance of the Prince of Wands in a reading may mean that a person with his qualities will soon be appearing in your life.

THE ENCHANTMENT

Close your eyes. Imagine yourself on a journey at night. You see a fire up ahead. You are attracted to it. As you approach, you feel the heat of the fiercely blazing logs. Look around. What does this brightly flickering light illuminate? How do you feel when you gaze directly into its intensity? Who else is nearby that you can share this opportunity with? Take note of this experience and open your eyes.

QUEEN OF WANDS

THE DREAM

The magnetic, self-confident Queen of Wands is wearing a wreath of flame-colored flowers around her dark hair, with a fiery feather tucked into it. These may be mementos of a walk out-of-doors as she is fond of the country and country pursuits. She is also to be found engaging in vigorous and healthy sports. The Queen of Wands is never too busy to take up arms for a good cause, although she can be blunt and impatient with those who fail to see things her way. Still, if you enlist her help, you will have won an energetic champion if a somewhat bossy and domineering one. Her basic nature is generous and loyal and her energy flow is steady, unlike her daughter, whose spark is easily dissipated. Men admire the Queen of Wands' excellent business capabilities and good money management. They respect her, but are not sexually drawn to her, in spite of her fiery, passionate nature. Perhaps it is her willfulness and lack of tact that they find unappealing. Still, she is a great nurturer of inspiration and they depend upon her blessings and advice.

THE AWAKENING

Act in the manner of an authoritative and self-assured person who knows how to initiate action. Prepare to be inspired in the near future. You need to be involved in a creative project that will hold your steady attention. You may be prone to bouts of anger and intensity but can be just as generous and radiantly charismatic as long as your self-expression is not opposed. Be aware that the appearance of the Queen of Wands in a reading may mean that a person with her qualities will soon be appearing in your life.

THE ENCHANTMENT

Prepare a hot, spicy cup of ginger tea. Sit where you can gaze outdoors. As you sip your tea, think of a project that you feel intensely about. Be spontaneous and imagine the potentials as creative inspirations come to your mind. Your passions will become heated by this exercise and you will soon know what action to initiate.

KING OF WANDS

THE DREAM

The King of this fiery realm is the perfect partner for his Queen. Like her, he revels in country pursuits and vigorous sports. He is even more sure of the rightness of his convictions. He is a somewhat more mature person and a great lover of tradition and family life. He is a benevolent autocrat and will attempt to dominate others because he is sure he knows what is best for all. Still, he is always the country gentleman and is loyal and generous to those he cares about. In fact, he scorns any kind of pettiness, meanness or lack of generosity. The shining, golden sun behind him symbolizes his masculine energy and dynamism, while the red butterflies hovering on either side represent flashes of intuition. A proud man, he may at times be arrogant or hot-tempered which sometimes leads him to gamble and take chances. In spite of these momentary aberrations, he is a noble, honest, and dependable man.

THE AWAKENING

Like the King of Wands, you are developing the art of taking action where power and pride are concerned. Don't impulsively rush into situations, and you will be able to simultaneously handle a great many. Adopt a warm and confident approach and go forward as a decisive leader. Be aware that the appearance of the King of Wands in a reading may mean that a person with his qualities will soon be appearing in your life.

THE ENCHANTMENT

Reward yourself by going out in the countryside when the sun is at its peak. If it is winter time then sit by a window where the sun's light shines through. Feel the energy of its rays, the source of all life. Engage in a recreation that you are skilled in, perhaps playing with a member of your family. Before you begin, think of the King of Wands and the qualities that make him who he is. He will give you the energy and ability to do your best and enjoy your accomplishments as royalty should.

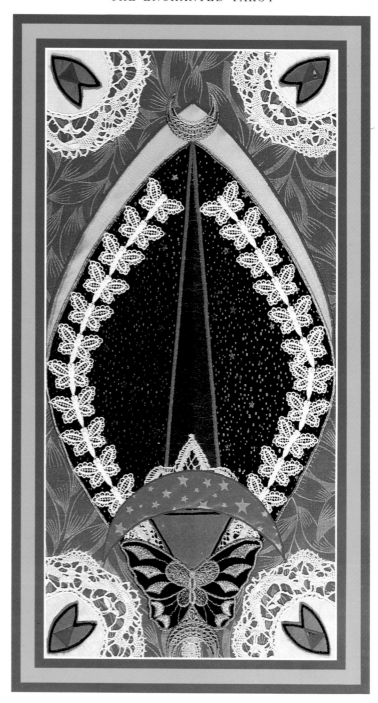

ACE OF SWORDS
FORCE

THE DREAM

Under an azure sky, in the realm of Air, the forces of truth and justice have triumphed. The raised sword conveys the message that adversity and doubt can be conquered through effort. The element of the suit of Swords is Air, or the element of ideas, and this victory represents also the power of the mind to prevail over uncertainty. Twenty-two white butterflies (twenty-two being a sacred number in the art of Numerology, and the number of cards in the Major Arcana) symbolize that all resources have been joined to reach the pinnacle of the sword. The waning and waxing crescent moons at the sword's base and tip show that a completely new phase of action is beginning; a phase of expansion. The large butterfly at the bottom of the card symbolizes the ability of ideas to move through Air. In the corner are four shields representing the protection afforded by mental powers. Behind the sword is a shape resembling a spade, the unifying background shape on all the cards of the suit of Swords.

THE AWAKENING

Make long-term goals and initiate them immediately. Some destruction may be necessary to cut away dead wood but do not use force or manipulation. If you do use this powerful force for unjust manipulation or punishment, Karma, or the law of cause and effect, will determine your destiny. This card can be seen as a two-edged sword, capable of both attack and defense. Concentrate on principles and not on form.

THE ENCHANTMENT

Begin a new project with this prayer: *"Angel of the realm of Air, Your blazing sword sweeps aside my enemies, and your truth drives away the shadows of doubt. Help me to be brave, and to triumph today and tomorrow."*

TWO OF SWORDS
BALANCE

THE DREAM

The clouds are parting in the night sky, as a figure approaches bearing a white feather as a flag of truce. One of her feet is poised on the central petal of the flower below her – a point upon which she may balance, but only for a moment. She is taking a brief respite before the clouds roll in again. She has come to this sacred place, now that conflict has abated, to reflect upon what has happened. Peace has been restored but some tension remains between the up-thrust swords. Will there be a stalemate or a new balance? A breeze has arisen, to blow away all sense of recent confrontation, parting both clouds and swords. The gentle figure appears diplomatic, without a trace of judgment. The moon, symbol of the goddess who cares for all, watches peacefully overhead. Although achieving such equilibrium can be difficult, harmony can be achieved by calming and stilling the mind, to leave time and space for mature consideration.

THE AWAKENING

Although you must be on guard to prevent time spent in contemplation from being a period of stalemate or procrastination, this is a time for considering the viewpoints held by others. Compromise is at the heart of diplomacy, and through diplomacy much may be won that cannot be gained through aggression. Though you may not possess all the pieces of the puzzle, for the time being, let things stand as they are.

THE ENCHANTMENT

Repeat these phrases as often as necessary when you lack direction or feel that you have suffered an injustice: *"I have faith the balance will be restored and my answer will come when I am ready. I am at peace with myself. There is no need to struggle now. Justice will be done in its own time."*

THREE OF SWORDS
SORROW

THE DREAM

Outside this cave of sorrow and loneliness, darkening clouds scud across the sky of a cold fall day. Under an inverted triangle of swords, a half-naked figure slides into a deep crevasse. Wounded hearts are enveloped by tearful black shapes that threaten to unite and engulf the scene. This triangle of swords has brought grief to the dream. Has a lover taken flight, perhaps with another, leaving the pain of loss, absence and the inevitable mourning for what might have been? The swords are pointed at the figure's bared breast as the ground beneath her rocks unsteadily. Filled with self-pity and jealousy, where can she turn? She has been idealizing a person or a situation and now the actual reality has led to this current disappointment. Life seems to be meaningless. Life can and must go on, however, and this inner pain must be endured as one lesson in a life of learning.

THE AWAKENING

There will be some realization of incompatibility in a relationship. Someone has destroyed your trust and your defenses are down. You are experiencing feelings of hurt and having bitter thoughts. Remember your true identity as a spirit in flesh, and your true purpose as a soul traveling onward in knowledge born of experience. Give yourself the love you have been giving the other and your sorrow will be conquered.

THE ENCHANTMENT

Lie down on your back. Close your eyes and relax. See yourself at a time when you were successful, joyful and content. Include as much detail as possible in this meditative state. If thoughts of pain or blame intrude, notice them and let them go. Remember that sorrow preceded many of the happy times and that joy can and will enter your life again. Believe that healing has already taken place. Repeat this affirmation: *"The past is over. I am healed. I love myself more than ever."*

FOUR OF SWORDS
SECLUSION

THE DREAM
In a place of seclusion and stability, a calm, centered Buddha sits in a position of meditation. He has retreated from strife and is relieved of all anxiety. The pyramid shape around his body creates a healing space. Clouds representing the confusion and pressure of the everyday world are parting, and all that remains is the purity of the connection to the eternal earth and the infinite stars. This is a time of grounding and re-charging. After the sorrow of the Three of Swords, with the hurtful results of too much attachment and self-pity, the Four of Swords shows a person withdrawn and protected from any difficult situation. By allowing the cosmic forces to flow through him, the Buddha has gained mystical insight. This period of quiet retreat to be alone with his thoughts has been needed.

THE AWAKENING
You have met this Buddha on your journey and he will teach you to look inward now, to accept and understand. In doing so you will be healed and renewed. This is a time for strategic withdrawal. Take sanctuary where you may find it and retreat in the midst of life's apparent chaos. Reflection, self-examination and meditation are called for. You will receive guidance from your Higher Mind after a much needed period of repose.

THE ENCHANTMENT
Do this for at least four minutes, one for each sword. Sit quietly in a relaxed manner, making sure that your spine is straight. Take several deep, long breaths in through your nose and out through your mouth, relaxing more and more as you do so. Continue to sit, breathing in and out naturally, being aware only of your breath, without thoughts or desires. You will find yourself becoming very calm and focused. This is the only result you need expect from this practice.

FIVE OF SWORDS
DEFEAT

THE DREAM

There is a violent storm. Lightning strikes sword-like at a gray, hooded figure with arms raised in defiance. Falling away on either side are protective shields that have been wrenched out of the figure's hands. The full moon casts a baleful light riding in the cloud-streaked sky, bringing a sense of foreboding. Defeat and even treachery create anger but do not necessarily rouse physical response; they can embitter the mind like a curse. A sense of weakness pervades this figure that has no armor. Blood edges the swords symbolizing that the figure must accept fate or be destroyed by forces much more powerful than can be imagined. Trying to cheat fate may gain a moment or two of time but it is an empty victory. The disaster must be accepted and understood as one turn of events in the great scheme of life before it can be used, as all experience must be used, to enable growth in the wisdom that is born of experience.

THE AWAKENING

If a problem presents itself in such a way that victory cannot be won or that the cost is too high, the fight must be surrendered. Accept this. Look to the future and remember that this storm will pass. Revenge or blame need not be meted out as this will just waste what precious resources you still have remaining. Where no victory is possible, it is best to walk away – if you are lucky enough to be able to do so.

THE ENCHANTMENT

Take in a long, deep breath. Consciously exhale, thinking: *"The wheel of life turns and turns. In this time of defeat I release my attachment to victory and plant the seeds of my future success."* Repeat this five times for five swords. As your body releases tension and resistance, realize that you are making room in your life for new experiences and victories.

SIX OF SWORDS
PASSAGE

THE DREAM

Moving away, at last, from turbulent seas, a small boat sails into calmer waters. Its passengers appear to be arriving at a safe haven. Their attitudes are relaxed and they can now look back almost fondly on their past efforts knowing that the hardships have made them stronger and wiser. The drooping sail suggests that they may have had too much mental stimulation, symbolized by a great wind – too great to be of use in their journey. In the sky to the right, there is a remnant of storm clouds. To the left, the sky is radiantly blue. Above them a rainbow shines, making the clouds glow with the promise of a new tomorrow. The flying bird carries a message of approaching comfort for a new land is near. This dream-journey can be seen as a rite of passage. It may not have been a physical journey but could very well have been mental, involving travel away from limiting thoughts, to the more productive thoughts born of a calm mind. The difficulties encountered during the trip could not have been avoided. They had to be faced and dealt with before life could proceed in a fulfilling way.

THE AWAKENING

A change of direction will give you a different perspective. A new vista may open up, bringing new, liberating solutions to old problems. A difficult cycle is now ending and the passage will be smooth after a few tumultuous waves of transition. If you can change your mind, you can change your world, for your world is greatly affected by your state of mind.

THE ENCHANTMENT

Visualize, in your mind's eye, a situation that you would like to change or move away from. Watch it change direction. Imagine that you have already achieved the new situation and empower your vision with this chant: *"Think a new thought, dream a new dream. This new direction will wipe the slate clean."*

SEVEN OF SWORDS
OPPOSITION

THE DREAM

A young woman tries desperately to escape a hail of seven swords falling from the clear blue sky. But on her face is a resigned expression suggesting that this terrifying situation was not totally unexpected and may, in fact, be of her own making. It could be the result of the things she has unkindly said and done behind the backs of others, or the limiting manifestation of her own fear of failure or even of success. Her movements are inconsistent, hampered by her own negativity and the mistakes that she has made in the past, symbolized by the black leaves closing in on either side of her. Though she tries to avoid the unseen forces intent upon harming her, perhaps her desire for peace is beyond her power; cunning and trickery may be her only way to safety. One of her hands is gloved and it is not possible to see what she has hidden there. Strangely, she chooses to ward off the swords with her bare hand while keeping in reserve the protected hand and whatever it conceals. This seems to be a rash plan as she may well fail if her wounds prevent her from skillfully using her trick.

THE AWAKENING

To escape from the opposition you are encountering, you must be logical and persistent and not resort to trickery. You must face the fact that troubles are often self-created and that only by identifying and eliminating repeated negative patterns of behavior will you cease to add your energies to the opposing forces.

THE ENCHANTMENT

To release patterns of your own behavior that are working against your greater good and highest joy, you must first accept the fact that these patterns in fact exist. Then realize that as their creator you can also destroy them. Identify them honestly, without judgment or self-recrimination, and then write them down on a piece of paper. Each day, for seven days, study this paper, make a plan to eliminate these patterns and chant these lines: *"Blow wind blow, blow a path for me. Make it clear and straight so the future I can see."*

EIGHT OF SWORDS
INDECISION

THE DREAM

A woman stands immobilized upon a pinnacle. She has reached a point where she feels that neither advance nor retreat is possible. Irregular waves vibrate through the air. They represent thought-waves of doubt and confusion. The rigidity of this figure suggests fixation, or the inability to directly face a problem, which is largely a mental creation. Her mind has been distracted by unimportant details and it now seems impossible to see the different options open to her. Although surrounded by negativity, she could cut herself out of this trap with the sword of deductive reasoning in her hand. But she must believe that action is possible before she can move. The swords aimed from the left and right of her represent interference, obstacles, doubt, confusion and misunderstanding, but the sword-like ray of illumination touching the top of her head is a sign that if she has faith, then she will be guided by a higher force that will help her to view her problem from a higher perspective. Though she is blocked, she can be released by her own powers and those of a higher source.

THE AWAKENING

Don't concentrate on unimportant details. Try to see the whole picture. In times of doubt and confusion, don't act immediately but patiently wait for illumination from your Higher Mind. Don't over-analyze; nor can you expect another to rescue you. Your own lack of perspective has imprisoned you. You must now work and pray to be freed.

THE ENCHANTMENT

Close your eyes, relax and cross your hands over your heart. Feel your chest rise and fall as, for eight minutes, you listen only to the sound of your breathing and the beating of your heart. Now call upon the Angel of Clarity to come into your life. Say to yourself: *"I now summon the powers of clarity to help me decide."* Sit for a while and experience your answer.

NINE OF SWORDS
NIGHTMARE

THE DREAM
In the night, a sleeping figure lies trapped in a dark, nightmare world existing on the edge of sleep. Strange demons, repressed hurts and childhood fears range freely. Worse than the sight of this chaos, is the feeling of being held in its grasp. Unclear forms alter shape, and circle in ever-stranger and more fearsome forms. This is a lonesome place, far from help and comfort. Shadows of pain, suffering and depression overwhelm the sleeper until she becomes a victim of her own thoughts and, like a martyr, repeatedly impales herself on their hurtful points. Her eyes are closed because she cannot bear to look at these fears when she is awake. The only way she can escape from these nightmares, however, is to open her eyes and awaken to what is really bothering her. She must confront it in broad daylight, no matter that there may be reputations lost, false friends discovered or the most unpleasant of feelings set loose. The alternative is torment.

THE AWAKENING
In darkness, personal demons seem larger than ever. The monsters must be met, identified and fought, in order to free yourself. Sometimes just admitting that such things exist may be all the knowledge necessary for your escape. If, as in a terrible dream, fears and frightening projections are not confronted, they may overwhelm you. Unchecked, they may even make you ill.

THE ENCHANTMENT
A solution may be found in your dreams. When you are ready to go to sleep, compose a one-line question or a request that specifically expresses your problem. Write it out and keep the pen and paper by your bed. Close your eyes and repeat your question over and over as if it were a lullaby. When you wake up in the morning, remember what you can of your dreams and write it down without judgment. Your answer will be there, if, later, you can read what you've written with an open mind.

TEN OF SWORDS
RUIN

THE DREAM
The worst seems to have happened; a devastating loss. Lightning has struck and an unconscious child lies in the arms of her heartbroken mother. This jagged bolt from the blue has, in a moment, rent the fabric of life, and life itself seems to have spun out of control. But above and beyond stretches the starry universe. The eternal silvery silence of the galaxies looks down and forces the acceptance of fate. Some things are beyond control. At a time of devastation and abandonment there must be endurance; living continues beyond personal destruction and the suffering is lessened. The hopes and dreams of the past are no more. The tears, grief and sorrow, and ruin may be the result of Karma but, difficult as it may seem, the woman can gain the strength to endure from the fact that there is always new birth after loss. No words can truly comfort here, only time and the new perspective it brings.

THE AWAKENING
When you are terribly afraid that things will not work out; that ruin and despair will beset you, you must "let go and let God." Accept that the struggle must end and blessed release will come at its finish. Healing a wound this deep may require outside, professional help. Do not attempt it alone.

THE ENCHANTMENT
On a starry night, go up to a high place with someone who loves and understands you. Look up at the distant stars and pour out your heart to them. Try to experience to the full any emotions that wash over you. Know that, like the stars, you are alive with a life of your own. You are an integral part of this timeless beauty. It is within you at every moment. Those we call "Saints" – the countless women and men who have also suffered yet "pierced the veil" of this mortal plane – have not deceived us or themselves. We *are* one with All-There-Is, now and forever. Ignorance of that is the true cause of our pain.

PRINCESS OF SWORDS

THE DREAM

The dark-eyed Princess of Swords lives in the realm of Air. She has emerged from her castle to receive a letter containing surprising news and some innovative ideas. There are no clouds to spoil the perfectly blue sky. Pink petals drift through the atmosphere and a white lace butterfly hovers like a messenger near the Princess. On her face is a pretty, child-like smile of interest. She is, to be sure, young and a bit naive. Sometimes she may say thoughtless and immature things, with a recklessness born from her infatuation with her own train of thought. But her mind is agile and alert. Any cloudy thoughts are cut and disregarded with a child's directness, and she is quick to discern the truth. One cannot help but be enchanted with her clever and intelligent manner and her liberal ideas. Sometimes though, in her quickness, she may get ahead of herself in speech and consequently the information she imparts may be misleading. And, because of her youthful heedlessness, she may be a gossip.

THE AWAKENING

Some interesting information will surprise you. You will be filled with innovative ideas concerning how to apply your theories to your world. Your ability to think in an abstract manner will enable you to see weak spots in planning. The ability to cut through extraneous words in communications will be of benefit to you. Be aware that the appearance of the Princess of Swords in a reading may mean that a person with her qualities will soon be appearing in your life.

THE ENCHANTMENT

If you wish to know the answer to a question or want a creative idea, write your request in blue ink on a piece of white paper. Fold it and draw a butterfly messenger on the outside. Place the piece of paper under your pillow. The answer or idea will immediately come to you upon awakening.

PRINCE OF SWORDS

THE DREAM
Below the galloping stallion of the Prince of Swords is a blue pyramid containing a white bird, the symbol of the Prince's land of clouds and sky. Under the stars of early evening, he carries his raised shield in anticipation of opposition and battles, usually caused by his imprudent and outspoken nature. He is young and quick to react and may strike out or be emotionally childish when he can't get his own way. However, he is a charismatic speaker, quick-witted and clever, and will probably manage to extricate himself from difficult or threatening situations without a physical fight. His bravery, even if sometimes just a thoughtless reaction, is to be admired and his philosophical attitudes are rather unexpected in one who, outwardly, appears quite conceited and superficial. Very active and productive, he will fight for a good idea, as well as for personal pique, and will usually be found on the side of truth and justice.

THE AWAKENING
Now is the time to respond. The Prince of Swords indicates a lot of movement, expressed as the interplay of all kinds of ideas and people with new ideas. Words will have to be exchanged but it is possible to forcefully express oneself without an argument. Be careful of sarcastic or cutting words that will provoke future conflict. Ideas can stimulate you now as they never have before. Be aware that the appearance of the Prince of Swords in a reading may mean that a person with his qualities will soon be appearing in your life.

THE ENCHANTMENT
With your eyes closed, imagine yourself floating on a cloud in an azure blue sky. Other clouds float by and upon one lies a book. Reach out and pick it up. What is its title? What kind of book is it? Open it to any page. What information is there? Remember it, for this enchantment activates new mental processes.

QUEEN OF SWORDS

THE DREAM

The King of Air's unmarried, older sister has a keen and perceptive mind that is of great help to her royal brother. She is a beautiful, dark-haired woman crowned with the butterflies of thoughts and ideas. She loves nothing better than to dance the night away. Despite this apparent frivolity, she is also familiar with sorrow and mourning. Unhappy, personal experiences have not provided her with great empathy for the unfortunate. She has learned that no comforting words or acts can change the fact that we all enter and leave this world alone. Living without a mate may also partially account for her occasional acts of bitterness. She is too independent and strong to acknowledge weakness in either herself or others. Still, she is a good counselor and, as an authority on many things, she is likely to produce a worthy solution for any problem presented to her. Her advice will be unbiased and fair although it can sometimes be delivered with a sharp tongue.

THE AWAKENING

Use your ideas and insight to establish your power and know success. The sheer volume of information to be considered at this time may be something of a burden in itself. Solitude is necessary to devote your full concentration to the matter at hand. Take care that strictness will not cause prudish or unscrupulous acts if there is any deviation from what is considered the norm. Be aware that the appearance of the Queen of Swords in a reading may mean that a person with her qualities will soon be appearing in your life.

THE ENCHANTMENT

This morning, relax with a cup of mint tea. Mint will increase your mental powers and open your throat's energy center, stimulating your ability to communicate. Sipping this healing brew, let thoughts flow through you and receive clear insight for the day.

Trust in yourself and your perceptions will be accurate.

KING OF SWORDS

THE DREAM

Bearing a white dove, symbol of his airy domain, the King of Swords stands among the clouds and contemplates his kingdom. His helmet is crowned with wings of maturity. He is constantly having ideas and lives for mental stimulation. Sometimes his thoughts lead him to daydreams and forgetfulness but his excellent problem-solving abilities bring him quickly back to reality. In dealing with potential adversaries he is diplomatic and clever but he never discards his weapons and shield. He is an excellent ruler and a recognized authority on many subjects, like his sister the Queen. Unlike the Queen, however, his modest and refined bearing will not permit either an air of superiority or arrogance. A thoughtful adviser to his subjects, he is a fine judge and critic. On a more negative note, his life is spent mostly on a mental level and he is perceived by others as emotionally cold and overly stern. This absence of emotion can make him seem ruthless or heartless, although he is always attempting to be fair and true to the theory behind his decisions.

THE AWAKENING

If you would be a master of the realm of ideas, remember that even if your intellect is aroused and stimulated by a flurry of new ideas, do not let it lead you into a state where daydreaming and imagining become more important than making your ideas real. Be aware that there are others who would love to share your thoughts and be stimulated by learning from you. Be aware that the appearance of the King of Swords in a reading may mean that a person with his qualities will soon be appearing in your life.

THE ENCHANTMENT

Reward yourself by spending a quiet and relaxing hour or two listening to some soft, soothing music. This will suit your aesthetic tastes as well as warm you emotionally. As you relax, imagine the music vibrating through you and flowing out from you carrying a message of universal peace.

♥

ACE OF HEARTS
LOVE

THE DREAM

A purple-winged heart rises from a vase filled to the brim with the supreme magical power of Love. This charmed vase is always full, for the giving of love creates more than its measure of love in return. As will water, love also takes the form of the vessel from which it comes and will only tolerate being cupped by an open, gentle hand, never a closed fist. Water also symbolizes the beauty of unconditional love, for its life-giving power is there for all to partake of. In all ancient esoteric teachings water symbolizes our emotions, feelings and intuition which, together, are the true language of love. In the center of the winged heart is a smaller, vibrant heart, clear and receptive. This heart is giving, nurturing, overflowing with caring and happiness. As at the beginning of a love affair, eveything in this dream is enhanced by love's transcendent glow. The purples, pinks and lavenders of all the Hearts suit symbolize the divine, spiritual quality of love. The heart is the unifying background shape on all the cards of the Hearts suit.

THE AWAKENING

This marks the fertile beginning of the flow of love into your life because you are accepting and receiving on a new level. There is a new opportunity coming into your life to experience the most positive emotions. Joy, health and happiness are being offered to you. Allow yourself to feel positive benefits flowing in and out of your heart. These are feelings that money cannot buy and time cannot take away from you.

THE ENCHANTMENT

To attract love, light a purple candle at the time of the new moon. Place a full cup of water nearby. Light a stick of rose or jasmine incense. Look at this card, the Ace of Hearts. Say: *"As I look upon this joyful, open heart, I feel the new beginnings of love and happiness flowing through me."* Be aware of how you give love and how you receive love.

TWO OF HEARTS
ROMANCE

THE DREAM

Two beautiful white swans circle in a calm stream among drifting water lilies. Mated for life, they symbolize the eternal unifying power of love. The differences of male and female are dissolved as a union is formed where each partner's experience is heightened because of the love and life shared with the other. There is perfect equality in the knowledge of both that they are special to each other. This card shows a romantic trysting place where lovers can meet without fear of discovery. It is a fairyland, far from everyday concerns and pressures, where love is cherished and encouraged. Here cupids and white flowers decorate the top of the large heart-shape and hint of a wedding cake and marriage. One of the smaller, floating hearts illustrates that love is written in the stars whilst the other, with its elegant and graceful curves, suggests joyful play and sociability. These two hearts beat as one.

THE AWAKENING

The focus of the Two of Hearts is on relationships, mutual affinity and union. This card represents all that is clear and true, supportive and comforting in romantic, familial and business partnerships, as well as the union and harmony of the sexes. There is potential for the development of a loving union and room for passions to grow. There will be a heartfelt emotional exchange of some sort but all may not be revealed now.

THE ENCHANTMENT

Using a red pencil, write down the names of two people who are to have a love relationship. Draw a heart around them. Fold the paper into a small square and plant it in a place where wild flowers bloom, chanting: *"Love in truth, truth in beauty, beauty in love."* Repeat this twice a day for two days. The goddess who loves all flowering things will help you and bring harmony and unity into this romance. If friendship results, know that this is the true essence of love. Be patient.

♥

THREE OF HEARTS
CELEBRATION

THE DREAM

Three dancers share in a spontaneous celebration honoring the love that has graced their hearts. They are the embodiment of Faith, Hope and Charity. Happy emotions swirl in the background and flower petals and ripe grapes are pleasurably crushed beneath their joyful feet. In the cleft of the large heart-shape arching above them are more grapes, symbolic of the heart's supreme ability to catch and hold the good things in life. The dance is welcoming and offers hospitality, inviting all to join in the merriment. There will also be eating and drinking, and a splendid party atmosphere. A radiant, positive feeling emanates from this dream. It is suffused with sympathy for those people who have been long denied pleasure and sensitivity in their lives. Friendship and the fulfillment of love's promise to heal is given to all who ask.

THE AWAKENING

Joy, creativity and happiness are celebrated here. You will find yourself filled with gratitude for the life you have. There will be a need to share your good fortune surrounded by supportive friends. It may seem difficult to concentrate on work in such a festive atmosphere, and your work may slightly suffer, but you need this pleasant time to grow emotionally. The art of sharing will help your work.

THE ENCHANTMENT

Gather together a group of your dearest friends for an afternoon tea party. Serve a delicious cake or some of your most mouthwatering cookies. Discuss joyful, creative and healing ideas only, allowing no disharmonious subjects to mar the tone of the gathering. Listen to some beautiful music. Lift your tea cups and salute each other with this pledge: *"Merry meet and merry part and merry meet again. The dance of life's more pleasing since I have you for my friend."*

FOUR OF HEARTS
RE-EVALUATION

THE DREAM
In a velvet cave a veiled figure has assumed a posture of prayer and meditation. The black box beside her contains old mementos and reminders of a past that may not have entirely satisfied her expectations. There may have been pleasures and material luxuries in her life, but at the price of unsuitable relationships that left her feeling empty. Now has come a moment of disillusionment and uncertainty, a time to re-evaluate her life. A spirit-crown glows on top of her head, indicating that this period of introspection and questioning of values is beginning to work for her greatest good. Now she feels the desire for a more spiritual love, and emotional rather than material satisfaction is her goal. This woman must face the possibility that she has never really known true love. She directs her ritual to the Spirit of Love, begging for her life to be touched to remove the gray pallor of a love without passion.

THE AWAKENING
When you are bored and dissatisfied with where your path has led, withdraw from distraction and examine your "heart of hearts" to gain insight. You can literally change your future during a time of re-evaluation. However, you should not re-enter the world of social activities until you are satisfied that you have resumed contact with a personal value system.

THE ENCHANTMENT
For purification, and to consciously separate yourself before the ritual from who you will be when it is done, prepare a bath. Turn down the lights. Add a cup of sea salt to your bath water. As you bathe, breathe deeply and say this affirmation: *"Though I may have lost my way, the light of Truth has saved the day. Now every day, in every way, I'm getting better and better."*

♥

FIVE OF HEARTS
DISAPPOINTMENT

THE DREAM
Love has been replaced by sadness and disappointment. Will it rain forever? Puddles of rain gather at the young woman's feet. The fan once used to cool burning passions now serves as a shield from the mournful raindrops. Flowers droop dejectedly and so does the disconsolate woman. Is it really the end of love? Three hearts are broken but two remain whole. There may still be hope. Love hesitates, heartbroken on the edge of despair, unable to advance or retreat. Her lover stands in the background, his gaze averted. Is he sulking or indifferent? She will not face him and knows that she must force herself to look out towards new interests. A seemingly harmonious relationship has been shattered. At the very least there has been unkindness and loss of friendship. With a long, sad sigh, she hopes that this moment of deep emotional vulnerability will soon pass.

THE AWAKENING
This is a time of deep disappointment but a conscious effort must be made to overcome it. You have lost love but gained in experience. Though feeling depressed and despondent, you must be as kind to yourself as you would be to another person in a similar situation. Like the flowers that are the universal symbol of love's presence, love can and will bloom again.

THE ENCHANTMENT
Pluck a rose and carry it to a garden or patch of earth at midnight. Dig a small hole. Say these words five times: *"Grief be gone, my heart be healed. For all my sorrow's buried here."* Bury the rose. Walk away and don't look back.

SIX OF HEARTS
JOY

THE DREAM

A scene of pure joy is depicted, taking a nostalgic journey back into childhood. This is a revitalizing and healing experience. No friends are as the friends of youth, where a non-critical innocence prevailed. Love was undemanding and it was enough just to be in the company of the loved one. Days could be spent in joyful play and time itself moved at a different, slower tempo, allowing things to be fully savored. All discoveries were unique. The world was new and as beautiful as a butterfly emerging from its cocoon. The Six of Hearts is an especially nice dream. Two children happily hold a basket carrying the youngest child as they stroll along. To go back and see and hear with the eyes and ears of the child that dwells within is truly a golden opportunity to renew a youthful happy and enthusiastic feeling. This feeling is always available but people are not always aware of it.

THE AWAKENING

This is a delightful, lovely card. By some twist of fate, a person, a feeling, a memory, a smell, touch or taste from childhood makes an appearance in your life. There is complete rapport. A feeling of nostalgia can be triggered by a gift or a short trip. These memories will leave you looking back at the time when adults – especially our mothers – were all-knowing giants and a year seemed to stretch for eternity.

THE ENCHANTMENT

Cut out a red paper heart the size of your palm. Write upon it this rhyme: *"Joy to you, joy to me, joy to everyone I see."* Place it on your mirror to remind you of the child within you. For six days, six minutes a day, try to see with the eyes of a child. Look upon this miracle we call life as if it was all new. It *is* new.

SEVEN OF HEARTS
ILLUSION

THE DREAM

A winged woman tries to gather seven brightly pulsating energy-hearts that have been caught on a net encircled by all the colors of the rainbow. Symbolized here are the worlds of imagination, inspiration and, most of all, illusion. The whole of the material world is represented as pure energy, trapped in the net of form and radiating an infinite number of colors, smells, sounds and other properties, giving the illusion that this interconnected world holds an infinite variety of all things. This is why the woman wears the wings of fantasy. She believes that this is the true nature of physical reality and therefore anything must be possible. In this dreamlike world she may become addicted by the glamour and intoxication born of illusion and may be overwhelmed by its implications, preventing her from functioning in her everyday life. Then she will be as trapped as the netted hearts. A magic shell-sun above her radiates the higher truth. She must face ultimate reality with her head to the sky but with her feet on the ground. Only then will her visions and the art born of them be of positive benefit.

God is a Big Dream Machine

THE AWAKENING

You may be daydreaming and building castles in the air. It is time to look at things clearly, to prevent yourself from becoming a victim of wishful thinking. You are getting to know yourself now and may have many creative and spiritual experiences. Just remember to be realistic about all possible eventualities.

THE ENCHANTMENT

Address your invocation to Lord Neptune who governs the oceans of our mystical imaginings. Repeat: *"Help me to see with my third eye of intuition, and lift the veil which creates all illusion. Help me decipher the real from the unreal, and guide my heart to truly feel."* Splash your face with cold water.

EIGHT OF HEARTS
SACRIFICE

THE DREAM

A melancholy woman cries eight heart-shaped, ice-rimmed tears which fall, like dried leaves, into the frigid stream below. Her sacrifice has been in vain and she is drained of all energy. This is a tale of love and devotion which has been denied and now serves no purpose. The fish swimming in the freezing water below symbolize deep emotion, but emotion that threatens to over-whelm and possibly even immobilize. To have given so much, uselessly, has rendered the woman as bereft of hope as the barren branches growing through the central heart. Like the illusion produced by winter snows, here it seems that life has been smothered forever and she cannot possibly endure in such a wasteland. Gone is the inspiration that moved her to the supreme proof of loyalty; to put another's benefit before her own. As the extent and implications of her folly are revealed, she stands momentarily frozen in her tracks, but as spring flowers are watered by winter snows, so will her tears nourish a wiser use of her devotional energies in the future.

THE AWAKENING

There must now be a retreat from emotional involvement. Too much time spent concentrating on the concerns of others, or on pursuits that primarily benefit others, has left you unfulfilled. You have given away too much of yourself. You may have to abandon that which you once sought, to seek something that is more worthy of your effort and sacrifice. You now have the opportunity to find a new direction.

THE ENCHANTMENT

Burn some sage. Hold a white feather in the smoke and sweep it up and down your entire body to cleanse your "aura," the colored halo of light-energy surrounding you that is visible to Kirlian photography as well as to some psychics and healers. Change the usual position of your rings or jewelry by wearing them on the opposite side of your body. Remember that your left side draws in energy and your right side releases it. This enchantment will begin a process of renewal.

NINE OF HEARTS
FULFILLMENT

THE DREAM
This woman is a genie who grants wishes and desires. Appearing from a ray of pure violet light, she brings fulfillment and satisfaction. The nine shining hearts surround her protectively in balanced perfection. The warm, red background is covered with hearts vibrating with the joy of already realized dreams and love. In her hand she holds a small treasure chest filled with jewels and pearls, a strand of which she holds up in an enticing way. She confirms that these great gifts are deserved and should be accepted without guilt or fear. There is nothing if not abundance in the treasure house that can be seen as the divine source. Partaking of its riches in no way lessens the wealth available to those who follow. The violet shaft of light as well as the lines of energy in the background symbolize the inseparable connection to a universal birthright.

THE AWAKENING
Satisfaction is achieved. Your wish is granted. It may arrive in an unexpected way or after a small delay but know this is a very lucky time for you. Be sure to wish for the things you know are best for you in the long-term because you are likely to receive them. You may know sensual comforts and a blessed period of contentment. The memory of this healing respite may be drawn upon if things become difficult in the future, thus helping you to attain the supreme goal of complete contentment.

THE ENCHANTMENT
In the dark of a waning moon, hold a heart-shaped piece of glass, metal or stone to your breast and think of your wish. Chant these words: *"Heart light, heart bright, what I desire feels so right. I wish I may, I wish I might, have this wish come true tonight."*

TEN OF HEARTS
SUCCESS

THE DREAM

Here is a joyous celebration with friends and associates, old and young, gathered together to mark their contribution to this successful outcome. They are there to celebrate what will be a long and happy marriage. A canopy of golden flowers glows warmly overhead, and the pale blue butterfly above honors and blesses the realization of long-held wishes for a heaven on earth. This is an emotional time representing the harvesting of permanent and lasting success, enduring love, wholeness and security. An ageless maturity is born from the attainment of true harmony and the contentment that comes with enlightenment. The young people know that this celebration is a harbinger of a life to be lived in the company of good friends and a loving mate. Those already coupled see it as a sign that the best is yet to come. All feel that this event denotes the crowning glory of a life to be well spent giving and receiving love.

THE AWAKENING

Under the bower of the Ten of Hearts you have found your spiritual family. You have attained a goal that will bring you lasting personal success and domestic happiness. Your reputation is enhanced, as are your relations with friends, relatives and business associates. The respect and honor of your peers has been attained through your own correct action.

THE ENCHANTMENT

Have a party! Share good food and drink; laugh, dance and sing. At one point have everyone gather in a circle and link hands. Take a moment of silence to be thankful for shared happiness and success. See the joy that is felt by all as a pulsating violet light enveloping the group. Now ask that all in the circle visualize this beautiful violet ball of light rising up and up until it reaches the sky. Then, with a shout for joy, see the light being broadcast out to the world for all to share. Then embrace one and all.

PRINCESS OF HEARTS

THE DREAM

The Princess of Hearts lives in a romantic kingdom by the sea. She is blonde with fair skin and dressed in a charming fashion with a large flowered heart upon her hat as well as a heart-shaped reticule tied with a ribbon around the waist of her violet velvet dress. She has a poetic nature and is gifted with a great empathy for emotional and artistic affairs of life. With a gentle and tender nature, she is rather dependent on others but, if called upon, is always ready to be helpful or offer comfort. She stands at the edge of a glittering stream and two fish are leaping by her feet. This water, the main element of the suit of Hearts, and the eddies of turbulence in the sky behind her, signify her emotional qualities and sensitive spirit. In her hand she holds a poem which may portend the beginnings of a love affair. Her messages are always from dreams and intuitions and signal new ideas, births and happy surprises.

THE AWAKENING

Something new, creative and loving is to be expected soon. Be sure you are not being too romantic and emotionally naive to make the best use of it. Or you may be indolent, lying around daydreaming when action is called for. Be aware that the appearance of the Princess of Hearts in a reading may mean that a person with her qualities will soon be appearing in your life.

THE ENCHANTMENT

Write a small poem of your own, "from the heart," telling a tale of romance, beauty and art. Lightly inscribe your romantic poem onto a seashell. Take the shell and cast it into water, either into a river, a stream, a lake or pond, the sea, or a special "watery" place near where you live. The waters will take your shell and return its message in a dream.

PRINCE OF HEARTS

THE DREAM

Across an idealized landscape of fair skies and floral pastel hues rides the Prince of Hearts. This prince carries no weapons but approaches all with his heart in his hand. His is a romantic nature which belongs to the Age of Chivalry, when knights rode into battle or went on great quests carrying the colors of their beloved ladies with them. As in the medieval Courts of Love, his ardor may proclaim little sexual involvement and may only be the declaration of a sensitive and admiring, true friend. Not afraid to express himself, the Prince often plays the role of artist or musician. His passionate interest in affairs of the heart may lead some to name him a Casanova but he cannot help these involvements as he is truly in love with love itself. He usually acts with good taste and gentleness. The heart he carries symbolizes news of the arrival of love or of a moment of intuition. He carries only messages of emotional import.

THE AWAKENING

Now is the time to be in contact with feelings of young love. The Prince of Hearts indicates a lot of movement, in the form of comings and goings of all kinds, of emotions and emotional people. Although usually light and charming and a welcomed visitor, he can sometimes be shallow and even deceitful, if his feelings have been wounded. At his worst he can be a Don Juan type who will not hesitate to kiss and tell. Be aware that the appearance of the Prince of Hearts in a reading may mean that a person with his qualities will soon be appearing in your life.

THE ENCHANTMENT

Try this visualization. With your eyes closed, imagine you are on a journey. You see a purple heart floating by in a stream. You catch it and hold it to your own heart. Feel it transmute all negativity in you into spiritual love. This purple heart brings new possibilities for intuition and creativity. Observe what you feel when you hold this heart.

♥

QUEEN OF HEARTS

THE DREAM

The Queen is literally crowned with hearts. Faithful, loving and imaginative, she is extremely empathetic with both her family and her subjects. She is the perfect wife and devoted mother. Every stray that comes her way will be collected and cared for, as she is a wonderful nurse and wishes to take care of everybody. Beneath her dreamy appearance, she is good-natured and understands life's ups and downs. However, she can be secretive to the point of deception if she thinks keeping things hidden will be for someone else's good. Her extreme interest and concern for others may lead her to meddle in their affairs. She cannot say "no" to anyone in need but if rebuffed, she will become depressed and withdrawn. She must always be on guard to prevent her desire to help from becoming a smothering kind of assistance.

THE AWAKENING

Now is the time to be aware of the less fortunate, and to nurture and care for them, helping them to attain emotional security. Your intuition is divinely inspired, for The High Priestess communicates most directly with the Queen of Hearts. This help must be given without expectation and should enable those helped to be independent. Remember the ancient Chinese proverb, "Give someone a fish and you feed them today. Teach them to fish and they feed themselves forever." Be aware that the appearance of the Queen of Hearts in a reading may mean that a person with her qualities will soon be appearing in your life.

THE ENCHANTMENT

Prepare a cup of rose-hip tea. Sit in a comfortable chair. While you sip your tea, think of some people who could use your love. Feel a surge of warm, loving feelings going out to them. Sending out your emotionally charged thoughts is a genuine method of psychic communication. Think about how you can express love in your daily life with a smile, a gentle touch or a helpful hand.

KING OF HEARTS

THE DREAM
The King of Hearts is the gentle ruler of this kingdom by the sea. His dramatic costume reflects his creativity and imagination but he himself has a quiet temperament. He is a good husband and father and can be relied upon to be considerate and affectionate. His presence inspires confidence. As he is, in a way, like a clergyman – non-judgmental and kind – people seek his council. His intuitive powers enable him to read the intentions of those around him. He is able to forgive all, even those who have made the mistake of taking his kindness for a sign of weakness. Always a true gentleman, he has a calm and mannerly demeanour. But this genuine self-control can be a thin veneer masking a fierce inner turmoil that can suddenly emerge if his jealous nature is aroused. Perhaps at times, his good manners prevent him from showing his true feelings. He has many dealings with the arts and humanities as he is appreciative of beauty. He is a great collector and has excellent taste.

THE AWAKENING
It is important that you make a sincere effort to be understanding at this time, appealing to the emotional aspects of the situation. You must be the ruler of your emotions by understanding them and not repressing them. Trying to bury strong feelings under a false surface of calm is dangerous. Be aware that the appearance of the King of Hearts in a reading may mean that a person with his qualities will soon be appearing in your life.

THE ENCHANTMENT
Reward yourself by taking time to quietly luxuriate in a bath scented with lavender oil, which will help you to be peaceful. As you relax, open your heart and forgive anyone against whom you may hold hard feelings. Extend compassion toward them and reflect upon the mighty healing power of forgiveness.

ACE OF PENTACLES
REWARD

THE DREAM

The very surface of the earth parts to offer you the treasure you have been longing for. Set in the richest vein of gold imaginable is the star of unlimited opportunity. This beautiful, shining, five-pointed star, with its glowing pink rays and glistening background, represents your wishes exploding into being in the material world. Its jeweled corners symbolize earthly riches that have crystalized from its fiery essence. "Dia-mond" means "The Earth Goddess," giver of precious stones and metals. The Diamond is the unifying background shape on all the cards of the Pentacles suit. At its heart is a reflection of the first star, the one we wish upon, and it radiates warmth, prosperity and security. The dynamic force of the Ace of Pentacles gives you the strength of the Earth to do the work to bring your plans to fruition.

THE AWAKENING

On an inner level, this card of good fortune bestows the great gift of knowledge and the materialization of ideas. For earthly benefits, this is one of the most favorable of all *The Enchanted Tarot* cards. Now there is a great sense of stability and earthly power. You will have enough resources to do and have whatever you may wish. Gifts or inheritances may be indicated, and desired material gains will be forthcoming. Your business activities will expand on a secure foundation. A new beginning regarding material wealth and practical affairs is at hand. If investments have been properly handled, much profit and wealth will accrue.

THE ENCHANTMENT

Stretch out your arms and open yourself up to the universe. Affirm with conviction: *"I deserve to be rewarded. I accept my worthiness by accepting these gifts from Mother Earth."* Standing with your legs shoulder-width apart, stretch your arms straight out at your sides to form a star with your body. Prepare to receive all the universe has to offer. Now hug yourself as a symbol of your self-acceptance.

TWO OF PENTACLES
CHANGE

THE DREAM

Two snakes – one light and one dark – writhe on a background filled with rippling currents of colored light and shadow. Soon the dark snake will shed its skin and appear light while the lighter snake's skin will turn dark. Thus is the ever-changing, cyclical nature of the material world. This is a world of duality: light and dark; male and female; young and old; life and death; each opposite being contrasted with the other to define its own uniqueness. The figure eight surrounding the two stars is a universal symbol for infinity. It is a figure without beginning or end; formed by a point that is constantly changing direction. The points of the four arrows, coming in from each corner of the card, dissolve at contact with the symbol, showing that every action, direction and possibility, present in every moment, is nothing more or less than another, temporary turn of events.

THE AWAKENING

With change, comes the growth that runs throughout one's life. The growth from child to young adult and from young adult to old age is meaningless without the accompaniment of the wisdom accumulated with the changing seasons of our lives. You have endured changes in the past, both comforting and uncomfortable, and are now being called upon to do so again. You must remain flexible and see change as opportunity, as you ride upon the flowing waves of life.

THE ENCHANTMENT

Use a crayon to draw a large figure eight on a piece of paper starting from the top of the figure and moving from right to left. Keep going over what you have drawn, without lifting your crayon, or your eyes, from the figure. Trace it again and again until the rhythm and movement flow easily. Now change and draw it in the other direction. As you draw think: *"I am flexible enough to adapt quickly and easily to all situations. My goal is contentment in all circumstances."*

THREE OF PENTACLES
WORK

THE DREAM

A sky, rose-tinted by the setting sun, is a happy harbinger for two women who have been working out-of-doors all day. Such a sky will certainly bring a fair tomorrow. The two women have been laboring together in a communal garden and their baskets are filled with fruit and vegetables picked at the peak of ripeness, and a few flowers for pure enjoyment. The satisfactory harvest has been preceded by shared effort and step-by-step perseverance. Black and white brambles and spiked thorns also share the background, and removing these obstacles to growth may have required much labor and effort. Obviously, with their relaxed stance and warm glances, these two workers are old friends and have developed the ability to persevere together. With fellowship they have worked hard to achieve the glad fulfillment that comes with the knowledge of a job well done. They have not wasted any time on the petty gossiping and jealousies that can spoil the productivity of the most dedicated workers.

THE AWAKENING

Though obstacles may stand in the way, look forward to achieving a distant goal. Work shared is work halved. Shared burdens are lighter; a friend or a fellow worker will be helpful. Satisfaction will be the reward of consistent effort with a partner. Do not try to do the job yourself. Choose only a partner who is willing to work as conscientiously as you. This is a time to roll up your sleeves and realize the rewards of tasks thoroughly and well executed for their own sakes.

THE ENCHANTMENT

Empower yourself with this affirmation before commencing a task: *"My work fully supports me. I choose partners who are successful, loving, responsible, and who get the job done. I am committed to my vision."* At work, toast each other to a job well done. Share a cake. Try to forgive any of your co-workers who do not have the ability to rise above their own prejudices.

FOUR OF PENTACLES
POSSESSIVENESS

THE DREAM

This young daughter of King Midas has worked alone for her material gains. The impressive display of diamonds and other precious jewels and fabrics spilling all about her has been acquired by good management and an excellent ability to place things in what she feels is the right order – with her needs coming first! Pulled from her opened jewel box, these visible signs of her accomplishments are clutched to her breast. Her face, however, does not seem to reflect happiness. She is thoughtful; maybe even anxious. Has she heard a footstep, or a door opening? Is someone coming to rob her of her wealth? Or is she thinking that all this is not enough and that she must gain more? Through her fear and greed, she will become the prisoner of her possessiveness. She will lead a lonely existence with material objects becoming the dominant force in her life.

THE AWAKENING

The lesson to be learned here is that real power cannot be won with increased wealth. Material gains will not satisfy your need for security in this world of change, because true security comes from within. You must reflect on the quality of your own values and self-worth, for these are precious things that cannot be taken from you, only given away, by your own thoughts and actions. Guard against selfishness and over-protectiveness. Your precious material possessions, as beautiful as they may be, are not always able to bring happiness.

THE ENCHANTMENT

Say out loud: *"I, (your name), now free myself from greed and suspicion. I will use what I have for the greater good of all, letting go of what I cannot use to allow room for new things to come into my life in a way that is proper and just."* Know that your success does not have to take anything away from anyone else. There is enough wealth in the universe for all to share.

FIVE OF PENTACLES
ANXIETY

THE DREAM

Outside a brick wall, which appears to be designed to keep them out, two ragged figures stand. Their clothes are patched and worn. It is dark and cold and snow swirls in the winter air as they stumble along the rocky road. Though the lighted window above them shines in an inviting manner, no comfort seems to be available. They have turned away from its warmth and the man is pointing out a distant goal to his companion, who is leaning upon him for help. It may take all their strength and energy to arrive at this next destination. They are a couple who have stayed together through many hard times. Perhaps they have just lost their jobs and are worried about finding new ones. They may have felt the indifference of fair-weather friends. His eye is patched; health may be of concern to them both. They are alone in troubled circumstances and must focus on survival issues.

THE AWAKENING

Though hardship rules this card, the couple has a certain valiant energy. You must not expend your vitality by worrying about the future but handle things day by day as they appear. In this way, despite hard times and poverty, you will be guided towards positive situations. This is a time of testing. If you can learn to understand and thereby control your anxiety, you will certainly be rewarded in the future.

THE ENCHANTMENT

Wear a loose rubber band around your wrist. Whenever you find yourself in a situation of panic, your breathing becomes agitated, or you are thinking of and blaming your mistakes on past behavior, snap the rubber band. This will bring you abruptly back to the present. Now repeat to yourself: *"I live in the present. I am safe. Life supports me and takes care of me."* Realize that the present is your ever-new point of power, the only time when you can make positive changes in your life.

SIX OF PENTACLES
GENEROSITY

THE DREAM

A confident and mature woman stands at the center of this card. An Earth Goddess, whose very touch heals, she is willing and ready to dispense the riches of the planet. The background behind her is strewn with discarded masks. Her generous, honest nature has no need of disguise. She believes that that which is given freely will return twofold. This "lady bountiful," highly respected for both her good judgment as well as her generosity, stands at the apex of her star. From her urn, the star upon which she stands and the full-blown flowers in the corner, flow glittering streams of jewels symbolizing both her charitable nature and material rewards. She is ready to share all the good things of life and hopes to inspire an equally generous heart in the recipients of her largess. She considers herself repaid in full if she knows her generosity will be passed, in turn, on to the less fortunate.

THE AWAKENING

Express your needs and others will help you answer them. Look deep within yourself and you may find the resources that you must share to know success. Fulfillment will be found through your generosity or that of others. This will be a pleasant, well-earned reward. If you bestow a gift upon someone, make sure that you expect nothing in return.

THE ENCHANTMENT

As you retire for the night, recite these words: *"Dear Earth Goddess, I look to you for help and as I sleep you will work to grant my innermost wish. I know that the more I give the more I will receive."* Draw a picture of what you want and place it under your pillow. Believe that the Earth Goddess will provide.

SEVEN OF PENTACLES
FRUSTRATION

THE DREAM

This peasant farmer's somewhat bowed figure suggests a certain inertia and fatigue. He has labored long and hard cultivating his garden in this barren place. The soil is rocky and, at best, it seems a poor spot. Evaluating the results of his efforts, he is disheartened. His project, started with such hopefulness, now seems blighted. The plant's sharp thorns have stabbed the fingers of the cultivator. Dark clouds have formed overhead and there is a trace of snow in the gray sky. Will an early winter destroy all that he has worked for? Projecting a fondness for botany and horticulture, this card also advises the necessity of the two most important requirements for such pursuits, that is to say, time as well as patience. Lessons are to be learned from both successes and failures. Good results take time and each plant or plan has an individual cycle that takes a specific time to be completed.

THE AWAKENING

Fear of failing, or indulging in worry about future results will not determine a favorable outcome. You must maintain a strong desire to achieve, even in the face of defeat. The roots have dug deeply into the soil and the garden will bloom again in its own time. Remember that it is neither profitable nor necessary to continually measure the growth of your project.

THE ENCHANTMENT

Stand in a garden or amidst some house-plants in the dark of the moon. Hold an apple. Say each line three times, concentrating and projecting these thoughts into the apple: *"As my plants grow, as the Earth moves and as the fruit ripens so I bud and blossom and receive."* Eat the apple.

EIGHT OF PENTACLES
CRAFTSMANSHIP

THE DREAM

A strong, young figure stands by a well-constructed wall of her own making. The wall has been built up brick by brick, with great attention to detail and a persistent productivity. She proudly views the results of her work with an expression of serenity, knowing that she has done her very best. She is obviously a disciplined worker, well-prepared and efficient. Her feet are planted firmly upon the ground. There is a feeling of centeredness and order about her. The flowers in full bloom above her head are both the blossoming of her productivity and its reward. This harvest follows order not chaos, trust not control. The skilled young woman is careful and methodical in performance and naturally intuitive in everything she does. She is the embodiment of craftsmanship.

THE AWAKENING

If you are prepared to learn as you work carefully, attending to all details lovingly, you will achieve great results. Be skillful and practical and you will become a craftsperson, doing work for its own sake and not for speedy self-gain or for others' profit. As you go about your task, think only about what you are doing and not at all about the rewards you expect as a result. You will achieve a period of serene contentment, following a job well done.

THE ENCHANTMENT

When preparing for good results in the future, pause while attending to one of the most minor details of your project and realizing its importance affirm: *"I use my special skills to add harmony, order and light to the universe. I am a patient builder, aware of the smallest detail of my every project."*

NINE OF PENTACLES
ABUNDANCE

THE DREAM

Here the garden is in full bloom. Everything suggests a flowering abundance and the pure enjoyment of earthly pleasures. The young woman, surrounded by beautifully cultivated plants and flowers and followed by a brightly colored bird, is a lover of nature and here she contemplates the rewards of her work. She has stopped beneath a sacred tree which blossoms with the promise of an abundant harvest in the future. She has earned this moment of relaxation and solitary leisure in the charming place that she has created. From the beginning, her feminine power has told her to follow her heart and to trust the universe to provide for her in every way. In feeling as one with nature, she has gained in most areas of life – in love, beauty, material gains and creativity. She has become the embodiment of beauty of mind and spirit.

THE AWAKENING

At this moment, you are on your way to being self-reliant and immensely enjoying the feeling. There is a strong sense of independence and freedom. An unexpected source may add to your income but take care that you don't also gain weight as a result of feelings of accumulation and increase.

THE ENCHANTMENT

On a Thursday, light a green candle as you think about Jupiter. Jupiter invokes luck, expansion and the flow of money. Place luxuriant flowers and a bowl filled with coins nearby. Stare at the flickering flame. Breathe deeply and repeat to yourself: *"I am open and receptive to all the abundance in the universe."* Feel the unlimited supply of all you will ever need that is flowing to you now and forever.

TEN OF PENTACLES
PROTECTION

THE DREAM
A person's home is their castle, and this strong, firmly-based building with its turrets reaching toward the stars is built upon a foundation from the past and the work of others. The enduring castle walls surround one with a feeling of heritage and security. A single, special pentacle shines protectively above, symbolizing that this dream is the culmination of the opportunities offered by the Ace of Pentacles. There is a sense of history and permanence connected to all this wealth, prosperity and material security. The gracious, formal figures below represent ancestral ties, rich inheritance and family tradition. Much is owed to the past and its values, and whether they will be carried on is a question evoked by this dream. At any rate, from this foundation a sense of security can be established to ensure survival and continuity. Precious jewels seem to float through the very air surrounding the castle like crystalized dreams.

THE AWAKENING
The first rule of any plan that would succeed is "Make your base secure." This card, one of the most favorable in *The Enchanted Tarot*, is a sign to you that, if you have done this and not taken shortcuts, your success is assured. There is a strong circle of support around you. You are emerging into a world that holds the complete manifestation of all you want materially, with happiness included as well. Retirement is possible and all the good things of life are available. Make conservative investments for the future, but don't gamble. Do not dissipate this wealth or allow luxury to make you lazy.

THE ENCHANTMENT
Say grace with your family at dinner. You should be sure that the menu contains at least one old family recipe. Repeat: *"I am thankful for all the protection, security and tradition that my family has given me and for all the support that I have received from them. Blessings on this, my family."* After dinner, everyone should recount favorite stories from as far back in your family's history as possible.

PRINCESS OF PENTACLES

THE DREAM

The Princess of Pentacles is a down-to-earth, practical young woman with strong values. She stands in her well-tended garden holding a beautiful bouquet of flowers, the harvest of her labors. Although a princess, she is quite willing to undertake hard work and get her fingernails filled with life-sustaining earth. Indeed, she seems a good deal more like a country farm girl than one of royal blood. Hers is the practical application of knowledge. While deliberate and diligent, she is by no means an intellectual, being unimaginative and, to tell the truth, at times quite a dull girl. Still, her careful and plodding ways, while not geared to quick action or management, will carry her far in material accomplishment. She will seek out only the information necessary to aid her pursuits, even if they do proceed slowly. She is always glad to help with any business matters or problems, and is a reliable and trustworthy person.

THE AWAKENING

You are learning, now, to trust your instincts. Become aware of the natural rhythms and cycles in your life that parallel those of the natural world of The Empress. The Princess of Pentacles brings news of material matters, helpful information and practical assistance. Be aware that the appearance of the Princess of Pentacles in a reading may mean that a person with her qualities will soon be appearing in your life.

THE ENCHANTMENT

One by one, on dried leaves, write down the things that you value most about life. Bind them together with several strands of hair from your head, tied together to form a thin string. Wrap the bundle in green cotton. Pray over them: *"I will work for my gain, I will learn from my pain, I will speak to the Earth, I will know my self-worth."* Bury the bundle in a garden.

PRINCE OF PENTACLES

THE DREAM

The Prince of Pentacles rides across his cultivated, fertile land. With his patient, persistent manner, he could probably coax a good harvest from barren, stony soil. Not possessed of great formal learning, he loves the land and all the things in Nature. He blows a golden horn to call his dogs after a day of hunting. He has spent a happy, beautiful time out-of-doors, where he feels more at home than confined within the gray castle walls. A stable, reliable young man, he is well-liked because he works hard and is a good provider. He does not experience great sparks of imagination and is perhaps over-preoccupied with material things. Being good with money is one of his strong points but it can also be seen as somewhat miserly behavior. Close-mouthed and usually serious, he can sometimes surprise with his robust, down-to-earth humor. He is slow to see another's point of view if it does not match his own rather narrow and conventional one, but he will be reliable and helpful in practical matters.

THE AWAKENING

This is a time to be stubborn and trustworthy in order to achieve monetary success. Concentrate on the physical aspects of the situation. Being physical, goal-oriented and competent can enable you to carry out your object with steadfastness and endurance. Be aware that the appearance of the Prince of Pentacles in a reading may mean that a person with his qualities will soon be appearing in your life.

THE ENCHANTMENT

Close your eyes. Breathe deeply and get comfortable. Imagine yourself walking through the woods. You come to a clearing. It holds a sense of power for you. Look around and smell the earth. Let the earth's energy rise up through your body. Notice an object lying nearby. Pick it up and keep it. It will soon be of service. When you open your eyes, know that at any time you can return to your power spot to center yourself.

QUEEN OF PENTACLES

THE DREAM

The Queen of Pentacles is enchanting, with dark hair and olive skin. She is a kind, calm and practical woman as well as a beautiful one. Men are very attracted to her for they know that behind her official exterior is a woman who is charitable and unafraid of hard work. She loves her husband and family and is interested in all they do. Fond of entertaining on a grand scale, she loves good food and opulent affairs, for she knows all the "best" people. She is a great patron of the arts and spends a good deal of time promoting gifted and inspired artists and musicians as well as theatrical performances of all kinds. She is also interested in the land as well as material things and she is careful about the details of all her activities. While not possessed of great intellect, she will share her good fortune with others if they are interesting and add something to her own status.

THE AWAKENING

Now is the time to be aware of the financial problems of others less fortunate and to nurture them, helping them to gain their own security in the material world. Your touch is healing for The Empress communicates most directly with the Queen of Pentacles. This is a sociable time but be careful not to forget that there is another kind of life beyond the social whirl of parties and dinners. Be aware that the appearance of the Queen of Pentacles in a reading may mean that a person with her qualities will soon be appearing in your life.

THE ENCHANTMENT

To attract, nurture and protect riches in your life, prepare a comforting cup of clove tea. Feel the beauty of the miracle that is your body; of the Earth of which you are a part; and know that you are secure. You are fertile, always able to create love and good fortune and as you sip the tea, remember someone with whom you can share these riches.

KING OF PENTACLES

The Dream

In spite of his warrior dress and glittering royal crown, the King of Pentacles is a jovial son of the Earth. He doesn't seek out the lords and ladies of his kingdom as does his wife, the Queen, but prefers the farmers who till the soil and work hard for their living. He enjoys animals too, as their unquestioning connection with nature is similar to the way he would like his subjects to be. He, too, has worked hard all his life and through steadfast and solid effort, has won a great estate and much success. Now he wishes to enjoy it and preserve it for his Queen and their children. Big-hearted and energetic in practical matters, he has no use for intellectuals and makes no effort to understand esoteric ideas. His only scholarly skill is to be found in mathematics because he finds the predictability and accuracy of numbers to be eminently practical in his affairs. In other ways, he is slow to change, possesses little taste and his social graces are fairly raw. He is truly a "rough diamond."

The Awakening

With a king's self-discipline and a solid sense of purpose, you will achieve success in your material affairs. Try to interact instinctively with all you meet and do not be confused by wealth or station in life. Maintain your ties to the natural world because this will fortify you in your dealings. Be aware that the appearance of the King of Pentacles in a reading may mean that a person with his qualities will soon be appearing in your life.

The Enchantment

Reward yourself by visiting either a botanical garden or a florist shop. Look around at all the beautiful plants and flowers. Think about the faraway places that they have traveled from. Admire their diverse shapes and colors. Pick one out for yourself. If you can, purchase a small pine tree to plant somewhere as it is evergreen and thus represents everlasting life.

THE ART OF
DIVINATION

The Major and Minor cards of *The Enchanted Tarot* can be used for divination, and three techniques for consulting the cards are given in this chapter. Interpreting the images on the cards using The Dream, The Awakening and The Enchantment given for each card, will trigger insights from your Higher Self. This is the part of you that provides guidance, and supplies you with the "irrational" hunches, intuition and flashes of inspiration that can make everyday life sometimes seem so extraordinary.

By shuffling and selecting one or more cards from the deck as you calmly and sincerely ask for guidance about your situation, you cause your Higher Self to guide you to select the proper card. Your state of mind at that moment implies a future course of events. Shuffling the cards as you concentrate on your question, links the question together with the cards you select to answer it, through the power of your intention. The two actions become connected in a meaningful way because they are happening at the same time.

The cards of *The Enchanted Tarot* can give you useful, inspiring and accurate guidance. You will learn how to use the One Card Technique, the three-card Three Level Spread and the eleven-card Celtic Cross Spread for divination. The best way to develop your skill in the art of listening to what the cards of *The Enchanted Tarot* and your Higher Self are telling you is to begin by using the One Card Technique and then the Three Level Spread.

The following instructions explain exactly how to prepare to do a reading, either for yourself or for others. They apply to all the techniques taught in this book. Always refer back to these instructions until they become an integral part of your personal *Enchanted Tarot* ceremony. It is important to prepare yourself before commencing a reading.

PREPARATION FOR A READING
To gain access to the tremendous knowledge of your Higher Self you must quiet the mind that "thinks" so that you can listen to the part that "knows". This can be accomplished by placing

yourself in a relaxed state using the technique described below. *Sit comfortably in a place where you will not be disturbed.* It is important that random thoughts about the events of the day do not intrude. In accordance with the teachings of Yoga masters, control of the breath leads to control of the mind and body, bringing them into natural harmony with the spirit of your Higher Self. Here is one method to achieve this calm, relaxed state.

Take a luxurious deep breath and, as you inhale, hear and see in your mind the word "inhale." As you slowly and gently exhale, hear and see the number nine in your mind. Repeat this procedure, but the next time you exhale, hear and see the number eight. Continue in this way, each time decreasing the exhaled number by one, until you reach zero. You should now be in a relaxed state and ready to formulate your first question.

Carefully phrase your question. The way in which you phrase your question will determine the quality of the answer you receive. It is best to keep your questions simple and direct and then approach your answer with an open mind. This will allow you to let the impressions evoked from the cards enter your consciousness. The more specific you can make your question the more direct will be your answer.

When you begin an investigation into a particular subject it is best to phrase your first question in the form of: "Tell me what I need to know about …… right now," or, "What should I concentrate upon in my quest for ……," rather than, "Will I get the job (partner, money, place to live, etc.) this week." Other possible ways to phrase your first question are:

"What is the course of action I should take with regard to ……;" "What lesson do I need to learn about ……;" "What will be the outcome of …… for (me, my friend, my family, my business, my relationship, my finances, my career, etc.)."

Once you have asked the first question about a situation and received information about the basic conditions involved, you can then follow up with questions concerning the timing of the event. *Suggest a time limit when you phrase your question.* This will clarify answers to questions like, "What conditions can I expect to encounter at work (today, tomorrow, this week, this month, for the next three months, etc.)," or, "How will my relationship with my partner progress during the summer season?"

Once you have become familiar with the meanings of the individual cards, be encouraged to experiment with your own methods of phrasing questions. Begin with simple questions, like the ones I have just outlined, and begin by using the One Card Technique. Once you are more familiar with the cards you can progress to the Three Level Spread. When your skill has developed, and you want detailed information about more complex situations, you should use the Celtic Cross Spread.

Shuffle the cards of The Enchanted Tarot both before and after your sessions, to purify the cards and prepare them for the next time. Some tarot authorities believe that you should never let anyone touch your deck other than to shuffle the cards for a reading. This is a matter for your personal choice. Many people also advise keeping your deck wrapped in a silken cloth of your favorite color, to protect the cards and maintain the energies established between you and your deck. Any gentle ritual that helps you to feel comfortable and confident about your readings is helpful.

Once you have purified the cards, try to visualize in your mind's "eye", the situation that you are asking about. If you are too emotionally attached to the situation, visualize The High Priestess, as you shuffle the cards and ask your question. Desire only the truth and not the answer you would like to receive. Shuffle the cards until you feel that it is time to stop. One of the many benefits of learning to use *The Enchanted Tarot* is that you will learn to trust your intuition.

To lay out the cards, take the shuffled deck and divide it into three stacks, from right to left, with your left hand. Reassemble them into one pack from right to left, again with your left hand. (These instructions are describing the cards as viewed from the reader's position.) Pick from the top of the deck the appropriate number of cards for the reading. Because you want to allow your Higher Self to guide your selection it may help to spread the entire deck out face down so that you have access to all the cards. Allow your hands to be drawn to particular cards, consciously choosing them for each specific position of the technique you are using. For example, when you are using the Three Level Spread, you might pick your first card while asking for information about the "past" of your situation, the second card while asking about the energies manifesting at the "present" time and the third card while thinking about the "future."

Lay out the cards face down, one at a time, and follow the patterns given for the various spreads. Then turn them over one at a time, interpreting the meaning in terms of the card's position in the spread, before proceeding to the next card.

You will find that some of the cards you turn over will be right side up, with the heading at the top, and some cards may be upside down, or reversed. Some tarot readers believe that upright cards most strongly express the qualities of the cards, but when reversed, they are weaker in the expression of their specific energies. Some believe that reversed cards indicate that their qualities and energies may be blocked, hidden or internalized. Still other authorities feel that the reversal of the cards makes no difference to the reading and should be ignored. I suggest that while you are still learning the art of interpretation, read the cards as their text indicates, regardless of whether or not they appear upright or reversed when you turn them over. You might like to keep a journal of your questions, noting your interpretations and which cards appeared upright and reversed. Once you have built up a record of your readings, you will then be able to review your interpretations for each card, in the light of its reversed or upright position.

INTERPRETING THE CARDS

When you turn over the card, or cards, that you have selected for your spread, pay attention not only to the words printed on the cards themselves but to any feelings that are evoked by the card images. Notice the colors, environment and attitude of the tarot figures. Let your mind "free associate." This term is used to describe the conscious mind's power to communicate with the Higher Self using symbols, or the language of the land of our dreams. Your first impression of the card image will create an image in your mind, and can inspire a further series of images connected and directed by your Higher Self. In a few moments, your conscious mind will understand the symbolism of the images and you will have your answer. This is the way of The High Priestess, and it is very powerful indeed.

The cards of *The Enchanted Tarot* do not tell you about a future that is immutable or "etched in stone." They offer guidance based on the state of your development and the conditions of the situation you are asking about, *at the moment that you ask.* Only *your* emotional response to the answer you receive and *your* personal decision to act upon the answer, will determine your future.

Using the Enchantments

Your ability to carry out readings will be aided considerably if you practice the accompanying Enchantments. There is no need, however, to carry out eleven Enchantments when interpreting the Celtic Cross Spread. Choose the one that you feel is most appropriate to your situation. The Enchantments add an extra dimension to your understanding of *The Enchanted Tarot* cards. Performing the Enchantments helps to reinforce your awareness of, and belief in, the unseen forces that surround you. Always perform the Enchantments in a safe manner. *Any small fires should be made in well-ventilated areas and in appropriately strong, fireproof metal or ceramic containers that will prevent sparks from leaping out.*

With their great beauty and timeless wisdom the cards of *The Enchanted Tarot* are always ready to assist as you take part in a ritual that is as ancient as the tarot itself and yet as new as today's questions. You are yet another link in an unbroken chain of wisdom that stretches far back in time. Approach all your readings with a sense of ceremony, sincerity and humility and all will be revealed.

The One Card Technique

Each card of *The Enchanted Tarot* embodies a very specific concept and psychology, and any one card can be selected as an answer to a question or as a meditative tool. Use the One Card Technique until you become familiar with each card, but even then this method is useful as a daily guide to your day's activities, especially when time is precious. When using the One Card Technique, if a single card falls from the deck while you are shuffling, you need look no further, that card is your answer. The following is an example of the One Card Technique.

QUESTION What will be the outcome of my daughter's relationship with her boyfriend?
ANSWER Justice

The appearance of a card of the Major Arcana signifies that this relationship is an important one. These two people obviously deserve each other. A striving for harmony and balance is indicated. By using free association, as I described earlier, the person asking this question realized that marriages in the United States are sometimes performed by judges known as "Justices of the Peace." The conclusion here, is that there is a good chance that this relationship might lead to marriage.

The person asking this question then wanted to know when her daughter would marry.

QUESTION Will my daughter marry within this year?
ANSWER The Hanged Man

Once again, the appearance of a card of the Major Arcana signifies that this will be an important year in this relationship, one whose effects will be felt throughout the lives of those involved. The relationship will be maintained at the present level. This enforced period of waiting will bring the couple increased knowledge about themselves and their relationship.

QUESTION Will my daughter marry within two years?
ANSWER Two of Hearts (but interestingly, The Hanged Man seemed to stick to the Two of Hearts and popped out along with the chosen card)

The symbolism here is unmistakable. The Two of Hearts symbolizes love and romance, combined in a joyful, lifetime union. The appearance again of The Hanged Man clinging to this card is an indication that the marriage will take place closer to the end of the two-year period.

THE THREE LEVEL SPREAD
The Three Level Spread provides a broader picture of a situation and can be useful for asking questions about the situations of people who are not physically present when you do the reading.

After you have prepared yourself and cleared the deck by shuffling it seven times, visualize your question in your mind's eye and ask to be given your answer on three levels. Shuffle and cut as usual. When you pick the three cards that will describe the three levels of your answer, lay them down from left to right and then turn each one over.

The answer to your question about a situation can be given in terms of its Past (first card), Present (middle card) and Future (third card) conditions or in terms of Mind, Body and Spirit.

When you select the first card, ask to be given a message describing the foundation of the matter; the conditions or circumstances that have contributed to where you, or the person you are asking about, now find yourselves.

When you select the second card, ask to be given a message describing the present development of the current situation.

When you select the third card, ask to be given a message regarding the outcome of the conditions described by the second card you have picked for this spread.

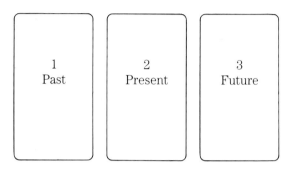

1	2	3
Past	Present	Future

If you find that the outcome is not one you consider to be favorable, you are advised to use the One Card Technique to request advice about how to obtain a more suitable outcome. Read through the following example of a reading.

QUESTION My emotions are divided between having a child and pursuing my career. What will be the outcome of my deliberations in the next year?
ANSWER

Past	Present	Future
Two of Swords	Judgment	Six of Swords

The Two of Swords indicates that this woman has experienced a desire to attain peace and balance in her life before making the decision to have a child. The fact that the image of the Moon, symbol of woman, nurturing, and motherhood appears on this card, is significant to this question.

The appearance of a Major Arcana card anywhere in a reading is a sign that this area of the reading is of great importance. In this case, Judgment appears in the "Present" position of the Three Level Spread, announcing that it is time to make a major decision, and to think beyond day-to-day affairs. It is always useful to read all the information on the page about each card and the Enchantment in this case mentions the word "reborn."

The appearance of the Six of Swords in the "Future" position of this reading indicates that a man and woman are moving away from mental turmoil into the calmer waters of resolution. The rainbow on the card is a hopeful sign of blessing. As with all interpretations, you should bring your feelings about the imagery on each card into your interpretation. In this case, the happy bird on the card was perceived as an approaching spirit of new life and the outcome determined by this reading was perceived by the woman to be indicating that she would be having a child in the next year.

Another way to interpret the Three Level Spread is through the levels of Mind, Body and Spirit. This technique is especially useful when used to obtain information about the effects produced by events of the past, present and future.

QUESTION What will be the outcome of my new job upon my mind, body and spirit?
ANSWER

Mind	Body	Spirit
Three of Pentacles	Two of Wands	Ace of Pentacles

The Three of Pentacles is an indication that this new job will create an awareness of the value of work that is shared equally with a diligent partner. There will probably be such a partner found at the new job. There will be no pettiness or mean-spiritedness to interfere with the attention that must be paid to the job itself.

The Two of Wands in the "Body" level of the answer offers further clarification of the Three of Pentacles in the "Mind" position. It is an indication that the function of the person asking this question will mainly be to supervise the actual physical work involved, and to concentrate on the proper distribution of the overall work-load among those working on the project.

The Ace of Pentacles in the "Spirit" position indicates that this job will bring a wonderful opportunity for spiritual renewal that might also result in a favorable financial outcome.

Although there appear to be no problems in this answer, you must always remember that it is the effect of the answer upon the person who is asking the question, that is the real answer to the question. For instance, a person who dislikes sharing work with other people or who is embarrassed when supervising physical work, might find this a challenging answer.

Once you become familiar with the Three Level Spread you may find it useful to clarify the significance of a particular card occupying one of the various positions in the Celtic Cross Spread. If a card's meaning, relative to its position, is unclear you can pick three more cards while asking for clarification and then reading them in terms of either the Past, Present and Future or Mind, Body and Spirit levels.

THE CELTIC CROSS SPREAD

The stone Celtic Cross is the unique form of the Christian cross erected throughout Ireland, and distinguished by having a circle linking the four arms of the cross, as well as scenes from the Bible and the life of Jesus carved into the arms themselves. Early Christian missionaries in Ireland used the carved scenes as visual aids in teaching scripture to people whose ancestors had worshiped the Goddess for thousands of years. The crosses were often erected near the stone monoliths that served as places for ceremonies dedicated to the Goddess.

The Celtic Cross Spread uses a cross whose arms are linked together by the circular development of the unfolding answer and a vertical four-card "monolith," at whose peak the ultimate outcome of the situation is found. It is ironic that the form of the Celtic Cross Spread, with a cross and monolith, symbolic of the supplanting of Goddess worship by Christianity, should have preserved both the memory of this event as well as the most popular form for using the tarot, whose wisdom is descended from the worship of the Goddess.

The Celtic Cross Spread should be used for the in-depth examination of a course of action. It not only predicts both the short-term and ultimate outcomes of a situation, but also gives valuable insight into the past and the present time, as well as commenting on how hopes, fears and the actions of others can affect the situation.

Once you have prepared to make a reading, select eleven cards and arrange them in the following pattern.

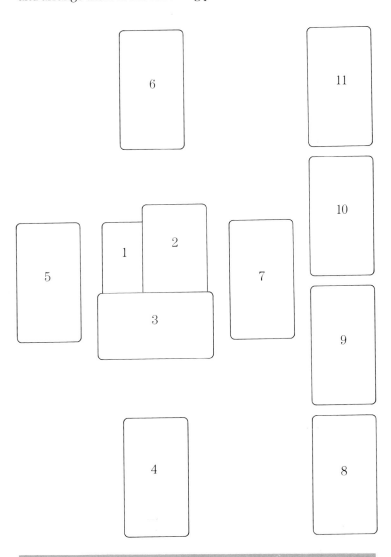

As you select each of the eleven cards for your Celtic Cross Spread, keep in mind the aspect of the situation addressed by each specific position in the spread, as described in the following paragraphs.

Position 1: *YOU* (also known as "The Significator"). This first card represents you and your innermost desires regarding the situation. Some readers select this card before shuffling the tarot deck, having decided that either The Fool, or a Royalty card closely matches their personality and situation. This practice restricts the advice the deck may offer about your situation. However, it is entirely your choice: you must decide which method is best for you.

Position 2: *What covers you.* The second card, which is placed on top of the first card, describes the present conditions. If the meaning of this card seems to reflect the result you would like to achieve, then you are in a supportive atmosphere.

Position 3: *What crosses you.* The third card, which is placed across the first two cards, describes obstacles, both potential and actual, to the achievement of your desires. It can represent a concept that is confusing you. Once again, if the meaning of this card seems to reflect the result you would like to achieve, then it is not to be viewed as negative.

Position 4: *What is beneath you.* This card represents the basis or foundation of the situation you are inquiring about. The situation rests or turns upon this factor, and it can have great significance when related to the short-term outcome. While you cannot change what affects the situation, you can look at and modify, if necessary, your attitude towards it.

Position 5: *What is behind you.* This card represents the past conditions and influences which have brought things to their present state. These influences are waning but their memory and effect upon past, present and future actions, must be taken into account and compensated for.

Position 6: *What crowns you.* This card represents the way in which you would like to see the situation progress in the future. This is the goal you should keep in sight as you work towards it. If the card in this position is a negative one then the elimination of either the negative energy in your life, or the quality of your reaction to that energy, are the goals that must be accomplished in order to achieve the ultimate resolution of the situation.

Position 7: *What is before you.* This card represents the short-term outcome of the situation. These are events that must be prepared for as they will soon come to pass.

Position 8: *Your personality.* This card represents how you must conduct yourself in order to achieve your desired final outcome. The appearance of a negative card is a reminder that unless you conduct yourself in a way that displays your sincere desire for mastery over life's unfortunate events, you will not receive the necessary support from other forces, to accomplish your mission. What course of action you take will greatly affect the final outcome.

Position 9: *How others see you.* This card represents how you are perceived by others, related in the situation. The assistance and support given by your family, friends, and co-workers, will determine the extra energy available to you when you meet the challenges involved with obtaining the outcome you desire. The appearance of a negative card in this position may be an indication that you will have to rely solely on your own energies to achieve your goals. You may also be misunderstood. Those who would usually support you may be withholding their support because they do not believe that the attainment of your desires will ultimately be of positive benefit to you.

Position 10: *Your hopes and fears.* This card represents your hopes or fears for the final outcome of the situation. The concept embodied in this position is a very important one; by initially considering this card as either a hope or a fear, you confront the fact that what may have been preventing you from achieving your goal is not only fear of failing but also the fear of how your life will be changed once you achieve your goal. The fear of the unknown is basic to all human beings, yet it is imperative that this fear be overcome before any progress can be made.

Position 11: *The final outcome.* This card represents the result of the entire course of the actions taken. It is the culmination of your efforts. The appearance of a card contrary to the final outcome you wish for, is an indication that you must question your desires, at this point in your development. If you are nevertheless determined that this is what you want, then you must ask for clarification of the actions required to achieve the desired conclusion. Use either the One Card Technique or the Three Level Spread to question your direction or to discover whether the problem is one of timing. The following example shows a reading of the Celtic Cross Spread.

QUESTION What will be the outcome of ending my established relationship in favor of my new love interest?

ANSWER

Position 1: *YOU.* Queen of Wands

In this case, the "querente," or the woman asking the question, chose the Queen of Wands as her Significator, feeling that she related most closely to the appearance and personality of this particular queen.

Position 2: *What covers you.* Princess of Pentacles

The conditions surrounding the querente at this time are those of a young energy engaged in the process of seeking self-knowledge. This card suggests slow deliberation, with practical, down-to-earth considerations being held uppermost in her mind. She is learning to trust her instincts, without at the same time being too impulsive.

Position 3: *What crosses you.* Princess of Swords

The obstacle here is that the querente has been unable to communicate her desires to her long-standing partner. She needs to be emotionally detached and truthful about her plans.

Position 4: *What is beneath you.* Four of Pentacles

The foundation of this situation is possessiveness. The querente desires security and to maintain her sense of self-worth, which may be derived from the material advantages of either situation. The situation turns on this point.

Position 5: *What is behind you.* The Sun

What is passing out of the querente's life is a sunny and bright domestic situation. The appearance of a card of the Major Arcana highlights this position, and in this case the querente is being alerted to the fact that she may be losing the warm and friendly support system she has known.

Position 6: *What crowns you.* The Magician

Her goal is to be able to manifest her desires in a more powerful way. Perhaps the domestic bliss that is passing away was obtained at the cost of the sublimation of her own desires to those of her partner. She now wants to be able to utilize all her skills and talents.

Position 7: *What is before you.* Princess of Hearts

In the near future, she is definitely going to choose to engage in her new romance. She is seeking a relationship more emotionally satisfying than what she has known. She will be feeling like a young girl in love.

Position 8: *Your personality.* Death

The querente must embrace profound change, eliminating one or the other of the partners to allow old patterns to fall away and leave room for a new future life. To continue to fear this change will immobilize her to the extent that she may lose both partners.

Position 9: *How others see you.* Five of Pentacles

Other people see the querente as someone who is anxious about the material considerations involved. This also indicates that she is perceived as having been with her original partner through hard times and her decision to leave him at this point could leave her out in the cold. It does not appear that she will be supported in her decision.

Position 10: *Your hopes and fears.* Two of Wands

Because of the meaning of this card, it is safe to say that it represents the querente's hopes rather than her fears. She has calmly surveyed the situation and is prepared to take charge of the direction of her life. She is confident in her expectations.

Position 11: *The final outcome.* Ace of Hearts

The outcome is love. The querente is definitely going to choose the new romance over the old relationship. This card indicates that she is beginning to give and receive love on a new level. Many positive benefits will flow from this exchange of hearts.

And so we reach the end of our first time through the book of *The Enchanted Tarot.* But this is not farewell, for, like the cards of *The Enchanted Tarot* itself, the information contained in these pages is meant to be consulted as often as you like. As you become more experienced in listening to the wisdom of your own intuition, as evoked by the cards, you will find new meanings in sentences you thought you knew by heart and you will find it easier and easier to contact your dream-consciousness with your waking mind so as to produce and experience your own vision of the state of enchantment.

ABOUT THE
ARTIST

Amy Zerner has exhibited her "Illuminated Tapestries" extensively throughout the United States and abroad in numerous solo, group and museum shows. Her work is owned by many prominent individuals and corporations and has received attention through major publications and awards including a 1986 Visual Artist's Fellowship in the category of "Painting" from the United States National Endowment for the Arts.

Ms. Zerner's tapestries are a complex blend of painting with and on fabric. She utilizes a combination of techniques including collage, appliqué, direct dye, beading and color image transfers. Rare Victorian trimmings and antique laces are juxtaposed with space-age materials and polyester prints from present-day rummage sales. By assembling and sewing these old and new elements in her pieces, she achieves powerful, timeless images that become "landscapes for the soul."

Ms. Zerner has been a practitioner of metaphysical studies since 1970. She lives and works in East Hampton, New York, where her large studio is filled with art, healing, love and magic.

ABOUT THE
AUTHOR

Monte Farber is the author and creator of the best-selling *Karma Cards: A New Age Guide to Your Future Through Astrology* (Penguin USA) and, with his wife, has created *The Alchemist: The Formula For Turning Your Life to Gold* (St Martin's Press) and *Goddess Guide Me* (Simon & Schuster). He is also a professional metaphysical counselor and lecturer, musician and film-maker. He has released a CD and an audio cassette *Good Karma* of his own compositions.

ACKNOWLEDGMENTS

Amy Zerner and Monte Farber would like to acknowledge their thanks to: *The Enchanted Tarot* team at Eddison Sadd Editions Ltd. – Nick Eddison, Ian Jackson, Ros Edwards, Christine Moffat, Elisabeth Ingles, Clare Clements, Marjorie Nelson, Maria White and Zoë Hughes and to Thomas Dunne, Pete Wolverton and Reagan Arthur at St Martin's Press for believing in our dream and making it come true; Sarah Daigre for her loving dedication, skill and assistance; John Reed for his good-natured persistence through our long photography sessions; Michael Triquet and Whelan Lace & Fabrics for their generous cooperation; Carol Sigler, Pati Smith and Carlie Feldman for keeping our energies well balanced; Frank Andrews, Leor Warner, Tarra Walter and Vanessa Talma for their advice, counsel and mastery of the ancient divinatory arts; Stuart Kaplan for keeping the flame of the tarot lit so brightly; Lucy Isaacs for her jewels and talismans; Linda Alpern, R. N., for capturing our likenesses (page 182) at "The Creeks" with thanks to Alfonso Ossorio and Ted Dragon; Lori Solensten, Daniel Romer and Richard Daniels for their loving friendship; the Farber, Zerner, Lind and Harth families and the many friends, galleries and collectors whose constant support has encouraged us to make art that is true to our ideals.
Amy would especially like to acknowledge her father, Raymond Zerner, for his loving guidance, her grandmother, Lilias Burten-shaw, for her sense of color and her grandfather, Clayton Spicer, for teaching her what it means to be an artist.

OTHER ENCHANTED TAROT PRODUCTS

For information regarding posters, greeting cards and other related products, or if you want to be notified of the exhibitions of the works of Amy Zerner, please write, enclosing a stamped, self-addressed envelope, to:

The Enchanted Tarot
Amy Zerner & Monte Farber, P.O. Box 2299
East Hampton, NY 11937, U.S.A.

Goddess guide me:
    How can I attune the energies of
my head and heart to best relate
to the following situation?

ate - State situation

    Answer:
        Head   )Heart   Home
        mind   Body   Spirit

Reaction to answer

Plan of action

Follow-up question
    How can I attune engies ofhead, heart?
to stay grounded during this process)

Answer

Reaction to Answer

What transpired?